When the Cheering Stops

Bill Parcells, the 1990 New York Giants, and the Price of Greatness

William Bendetson and Leonard Marshall

TRIUMPH
BOOKS

When the Cheering Stops

Bill Parcells, the 1990 New York Giants, and the Price of Greatness

Library of Congress Cataloging-in-Publication Data
Bendetson, William.
  When the cheering stops : Bill Parcells, the 1990 New York Giants, and the price of greatness / William Bendetson and Leonard Marshall.
      p. cm.
  ISBN 978-1-60078-382-1
  1. New York Giants (Football team) 2. Parcells, Bill. I. Marshall, Leonard. II. Title.

  GV956.N4B43 2010
  796.332'64097471—dc22

                                        2010016569

This book is available in quantity at special discounts for your group or organization. For further information, contact:

Triumph Books
542 South Dearborn Street
Suite 750
Chicago, Illinois 60605
(312) 939-3330
Fax (312) 663-3557
www.triumphbooks.com

Printed in U.S.A.
ISBN: 978-1-60078-382-1
Design by Amy Carter

Title page frontispiece: Giants Stadium (Getty Images)

To my parents and brothers for all of their support over the years.

—W.B.

To my parents, Leonard and Nellie Marshall, for providing me with guidance and courage to go after my dreams, and to my kids, for being my rock.

—L.M.

Contents

Foreword

IT WAS A RESILIENT CREW THAT STRETCHED the NFC dominance into the 1990s—battle hardened—with a combination of experienced championship players and an influx of youth and power.

A dependable defense that could play with a three-point lead. A power-laden running game that could run out any clock anywhere in the NFL.

It was a smart team, lightly penalized, that set an NFL record for fewest turnovers. It did not win by accident. It beat the threepeat-aspiring San Francisco 49ers on the road in the NFC Championship Game—and then stopped the no-huddle offense of the '90s Buffalo Bills in Super Bowl XXV.

It overcame the loss of their starting quarterback and got a good performance from their backup just when they needed it most. No one had ever won a Super Bowl with a backup quarterback before.

Their formula was simple but effective. Control the game physically and don't beat yourselves.

They had an all-star group of assistant coaches who have gone on to their own successes: Belichick, Coughlin, Crennel, Groh, Weis, Sweatman, Hoaglin, Handley, Erhardt, Pope, and Parker.

It was a championship team with a champion's heart that never cracked under the pressure of the moment.

This team could smother and suffocate—and much like the constrictor it emulated, it would never relax.

Author's Note

WHEN HISTORICAL FOOTBALL BOOKS ARE WRITTEN, authors and sportswriters often like to glamorize the past in order to allow fans to relive some of the great historical teams from our era. What we often forget is that an athlete exists beyond his jersey number and on-field heroics.

The average NFL career is slightly longer than three years. At 30, most players' careers are finished, and just about every player is out of the game by 35 (with limited exceptions). When I decided to write a book about the 1990 Giants, I wanted to write about more than just that storied season, since players spend far more of their lives retired than active.

The 1990 New York Giants team fascinated me more than any other in NFL history. It had all the elements: two legendary coaches in Bill Parcells and Bill Belichick; an interesting storyline, as two backups—quarterback Jeff Hostetler and running back Ottis Anderson—led an improbable Super Bowl run; and one of the most exciting Super Bowls in NFL history (best known for the miss "wide right" by Bills kicker Scott Norwood).

But more important, I decided to intersperse the exciting narrative of the 1990 season with stories of what happened to some of the Giants players in the past 20 years—illuminating the difficulties retired players face, from receiving disability benefits to the challenge of adjusting to a more sedentary lifestyle. Their stories off the field are as compelling as the theatrics of their magical season.

I hope you enjoy it.

—W.B., March 2010

1.

The Celebration

IT MIGHT HAVE BEEN THE GREATEST pressure situation in NFL history. Bills place-kicker Scott Norwood did not have the comfort of overtime if he missed. Kickers have won three Super Bowls on the strength of their feet in the final moments, but each came when the game was tied, with overtime as a safety net. On January 27, 1991, the Buffalo Bills were trailing 20–19 in Super Bowl XXV. Norwood lined up for a 47-yard field goal with eight seconds left. As the ball left Norwood's foot, Bills general manager Bill Polian uttered the phrase that all general managers hope to utter. Standing next to the opposing general manager, the Giants' George Young, Polian said, "We are world champions."

"I thought it was good when it left his foot," Polian still insists years later.

Before Norwood's kick, Parcells asked venerable tough guy and Giants kicker Matt Bahr about whether he thought Norwood could hit it. Bahr told Parcells that Norwood had never connected on grass from this distance, and that he was only one for five in his career on grass from more than 40 yards. Because of the humidity, Bahr also told Parcells that Norwood needed to angle his kick to the right—without pulling it too far to the side, of course.

Bahr might have been a sage, or so Parcells jokingly calls him, because Norwood's kick sailed right at the last minute. The Giants could hardly contain themselves. Safeties Everson Walls and Myron Guyton ran 50 yards across the field like synchronized swimmers, their hands repeatedly making the "no-good" signal. They almost never stopped running. Giants coach Bill Parcells jogged off the field with one hand giving his signature fist pump and the other

1

hand holding the head of Lawrence Taylor[1], the ferocious Giants pass rusher. Giants quarterback Jeff Hostetler held his two sons on separate shoulders, vindicated from all of the critics who said he couldn't lead the Giants to a Super Bowl victory.

For Walls, that missed field goal completed the best year of his life. He had always dreamed of playing in New York and his wife, Shreill, loved the big-city atmosphere. New York was where Walls "hid out" when he held out from Dallas Cowboys training camp in 1983. It's where he wanted to live as a 12-year-old when busing forced him to attend a mostly white school in Dallas, Texas. Walls had never won a championship—not in high school, not as a cornerback at Grambling State, not in his nine mostly losing seasons with the Dallas Cowboys. A lifelong dream was finally realized.

On the other sideline, the Buffalo Bills couldn't have been more disappointed. They were the best team the AFC had sent to the Super Bowl in years. There was a feeling that this Bills team was destined to be *the* team of the 1990s like the Pittsburgh Steelers had been to the 1970s and the San Francisco 49ers to the 1980s. Even though the Giants and Bills finished with identical regular season records at 13–3, the Giants limped into the playoffs (3–3 in their last six games). The Bills, firing on all cylinders, handily defeated their two playoff opponents. Most notable was their 51–3 thumping of the Los Angeles Raiders in the AFC Championship Game, with Al Davis shaking his head in the visiting owner's box as Buffalo seemed on the verge of a dynasty. Defensive coordinators marveled at the Bills' high-flying offense and few had an answer to it. They tried everything. Some Raiders players joked that prayer might be the best way to stop the Bills.

Bills linebacker Darryl Talley was the first to approach Norwood after he missed the kick that would have given Buffalo the Super Bowl victory. Talley always respected Norwood, and he remembered how many cold-weather games the Bills won because of his heroics. Talley told him, "We'll get 'em next year."

[1] Hereinafter "LT" will refer to Lawrence Taylor

"That's all you really could say. There was no sense in crying about it. I knew we had a really good team and I thought we would be back," Talley said.

Talley hasn't watched a tape of the game since—he, like many Bills players, prefers that fans remember the distinction of qualifying for four straight Super Bowls as opposed to the losses in all four.

Giants players, though, love to reminisce about Bill Belichick's strategy and the big plays they made—discussing their high third-down productivity, both on offense and defense. The Bills, like any losing team, will quietly acknowledge their mistakes. Talley still thinks about missing tackles on Dave Meggett or Mark Ingram in the third quarter—tackles that could have stopped what became the longest touchdown drive in Super Bowl history. Walls is far more jovial when he recalls how Perry Williams decked Bills wide receiver Al Edwards on third down of the Bills' penultimate possession to prevent them from picking up a first down on third-and-8.

Bills coach Marv Levy said little in the locker room after the game. He refused to blame Norwood for the loss in a postgame interview with ABC's Lynn Swann. It was one of the reasons players loved Marv Levy. He believed in that old-fashioned adage, "You win as a team, you lose as a team." He never blamed any one player for a loss. To this day, Levy reiterates the phrase he said after the game and probably a thousand times since: "It should not have come down to Scott's kick." Talley agrees.

Levy could have harped on the Bills' poor third-down performance—failing to convert on third down until their last drive, yet allowing the Giants to convert nine of 16 third-down attempts. He could also enumerate the multitude of dropped passes or the absence of a pass rush. Instead, he told his team, "There is not a loser in the room," even though he was clearly disappointed with the team's loss. Norwood could barely say anything to Swann other than the standard "I let my team down and I will come back next year."

Only about half an hour earlier, ABC play-by-play announcer Al Michaels had an eerie premonition as the Bills trailed the Giants 20–19 with 2:16 remaining at their own 10. Giants punter Sean Landeta nailed another high-spiraling 38-yard punt that stayed in the air for about five seconds, causing Bills wide receiver Al Edwards to make his fourth fair catch of the day. Parcells thought Landeta's ability to continuously pin the Bills deep in their own territory was a major factor in the Giants victory. Michaels told Frank Gifford and Dan Dierdorf in the booth that Buffalo Bills kicker Scott Norwood was only 1-for-5 on kicks of 40 yards or more on grass.

It was the type of odd statistic that can make sports fans cringe—another example of a broadcast crew trying to show off the hours of research that go into a telecast. We have all heard 'em and often want to tell the announcers to leave us alone. But somehow, this one was different.

With the Giants dropping seven or eight into coverage on almost every play, the Bills couldn't expect to connect on any long passes. The sure-handed Andre Reed had already dropped four passes, more drops than he seemingly had in the entire regular season. Giants linebackers leveled Reed every time he touched the ball, causing him to drop even easy passes. Reed lost a third-and-1 pass over the middle in the second quarter, afraid of an oncoming hit from Giants linebacker Pepper Johnson. Critics could point to this one game as a primary reason why Reed is not in the Hall of Fame. If Reed had caught the passes he normally caught, the Bills would probably have been Super Bowl champions and Reed might be a Hall of Famer.

"He played like a softie," Walls said.

The Bills had only one timeout, plus the two-minute warning, to get into field-goal range. It wasn't going to be easy. Dan Dierdorf appropriately joked that at least the Bills were used to the no-huddle offense. Unlike most teams, the Bills didn't have their offensive coordinator relay the plays in to the quarterback, they let the quarterback call his own plays. Quarterback Jim Kelly came to the line, screamed a certain phrase to indicate a formation, then followed it with another to indicate the passing or running package out of that formation.

"A quarterback's dream," noted Dierdorf during the broadcast.

The Bills were the better team, and this drive was a chance to escape with a win. It was what good teams were supposed to do, coaches famously say: win when you don't play your best.

The Giants defense was well rested, relative to the average game. New York's offense had held the ball for 40 minutes and 33 seconds, a Super Bowl record. At one point, the Giants defense stayed on the bench for a full hour as the Giants offense completed two clock-killing touchdown drives on either side of the half. The participants in the 1990 Super Bowl halftime show had spent more time on the field than Kelly and the Bills offense. Still, what ensued was a dramatic finish that was unforgettable and heartbreaking.

Walls remained positive on the last drive, believing in equal and opposite reactions, the yin and the yang. He believes God gives you experiences to balance yourself out. Nine years earlier, Walls was covering the 49ers with wide receiver Dwight Clark on maybe the most memorable play in NFL history, when Clark made what is simply referred to as "the Catch"—a leaping mid-air grab of a high Joe Montana floater—clinching the NFC championship over the Cowboys and catapulting the 49ers to their first of four Super Bowls. Walls remembers looking back at Montana because the pass stayed in the air so long that he thought it might go over his head. By the time he turned around the ball was in Clark's hands.

That was the closest Walls had ever come to winning a championship. Now, with Super Bowl XXV within reach, he wanted to think positive—but he couldn't help but think about "the Catch."

"I told myself, *Don't think you are receding.*"

Nonetheless, that very thought entered Walls' head on the final drive. The Giants shut down the Bills' passing game, just as they had all night. But Jim Kelly showed true grit, finding a way to scramble despite the fact that he wasn't the most athletic quarterback. That grittiness showed on the first play when the Bills lined up with three wide receivers, covered perfectly by the Giants, and Kelly still scrambled for eight yards.

"It was frustrating because you think you are doing everything right and then he scrambles. There was really nothing we could do," Walls said.

That play stopped the clock at the two-minute warning. On second down, the receivers were once again covered, so Kelly was forced to scramble again. This time, he gained only a yard and a half.

It was a little-known secret, something that seemed obvious with hindsight, but remained unclear to many defensive coordinators when the Giants prepared for Buffalo. Defensive coordinator Bill Belichick, young and well groomed at the time, noticed that almost every time Kelly lined up under center the Bills ran the ball. It was a signal to the Giants that they needed to line up in their base defense, as opposed to their third-down defense, which they had played on almost every snap. Buffalo, however, stayed in the shotgun, lining up in a three-wide-receiver, one-back set. The Bills often threw on third-and-short—usually a crossing pattern to Andre Reed. But that had failed to work all night. Buffalo still lined up in a three wide receiver one back set to give the illusion of a pass.

"With Bill Parcells motivating us and with Bill Belichick designing our defenses, we knew that we were never going to be outcoached," said LT.

Kent Hull, the center, made a direct snap to Kelly. Buffalo called a run to the left side—an area with holes in the Giants zone. The strength of the Bills offensive line was also on the left side with Hull, guard Jim Ritcher, and tackle Will Wolford. They easily pulled Taylor, Johnson, and Erik Howard toward the center of the line as Thurman Thomas sprinted to the left for 22 yards. Walls, who came from the middle of the field, was able to reach his arms around Thomas' legs and make the game-saving tackle. Parcells called it the most critical play of the game, because if Walls hadn't made that tackle, Thomas probably would have gone all the way. The Bills called their last timeout.

LT mentioned to ABC's Brent Musburger during the postgame celebration that a key to the Giants' success was taking Thurman Thomas out of the passing game. Belichick had a linebacker or defensive lineman shadow Thomas on

6

almost every play. Leonard Marshall or Johnson hit Thomas before they rushed the passer to disrupt the rhythm of the Bills timing offense—a similar strategy was implemented against St. Louis Rams running back Marshall Faulk 11 years later when the New England Patriots beat the Rams in Super Bowl XXXVI.

Reed hung onto a four-yard pass before Carl Banks laid him out, preventing him from making an upfield move. The Bills quickly came to the line of scrimmage. Once again, all the Bills receivers were covered, so Kelly scrambled nine yards to the Giants 46, New York preventing any passes to the outside. The Bills had no timeouts left, so the last thing the Giants wanted was for the Bills to get out of bounds.

Tight end Keith McKeller made a circuslike shoe-top catch for six yards to get to the Giants 40. On the next play, the Bills offensive line forced the Giants defensive line to the left as Thomas exploded for 10 yards to the right with Everson Walls coming from the opposite side of the field to make the tackle at the Giants 29. He attributes the tackle to his attitude of never giving up, as Walls, one of the slowest men on the field, tripped up Thomas, one of the fastest guys.

"I realized that if I didn't make the tackle, he was gone," Walls said. "We also knew that Scott wasn't a great kicker on grass from long range, so even if Thomas gains five or 10 more yards, that could have been the difference."

The Bills, out of timeouts, had little choice but to spike the football. Giants offensive lineman Bob Kratch stood with his teammates and only thought the worst. He imagined Norwood making the kick, partly because Giants kicker Matt Bahr told Kratch that despite Norwood's struggles on grass, he liked his chances in the clutch. Many Giants players were surprisingly content either way, realizing that no one had expected the game to be this close.

"I remember thinking there was nothing we could really hang our heads about," said Giants center Bart Oates. "Particularly on offense, a lot of people thought we executed our game plan to perfection. We also knew the Giants defense was exhausted because of the warm temperatures and high humidity. We knew they had done the best they could."

Norwood missed the 47-yard kick wide right and the Giants ran onto the field. ABC sideline reporter Lynn Swann had the unenviable task of interviewing Norwood in the locker room. Swann handled the assignment with class—Norwood needed little reminder of the obvious that if he had made the kick, the Bills would be Super Bowl champions. Norwood was stoic—all he mumbled was, "I let the team down."

The postgame locker room scene for the Giants could not have been more joyous. Musburger delivered the Vince Lombardi trophy to Bill Parcells, who paid his team the ultimate compliment.

"I don't think our team could have played better," he said—also acknowledging that the Giants had some luck on their side. "Both teams fought valiantly. If the two teams played tomorrow, the score could have been 20–19 in favor of Buffalo."

2.

Turmoil to Dominance

AMONG THE NOISE HERALDING THE BUFFALO BILLS as six-point favorites in Super Bowl XXV, it is often forgotten that for most of the 1990 season, it was the Giants, along with the San Francisco 49ers, that were considered the two best teams in football. During the middle of the season, *New York Daily News* NFL columnist Gary Myers sarcastically suggested that maybe the NFL should just cancel the playoffs and have the 49ers square off against the Giants for the championship. Both teams started their seasons 10–0.

Before the Giants could worry about their first game against their arch nemesis Philadelphia Eagles, they had to fix their own in-house mess. There were numerous holdouts, mostly on the defensive side, during training camp. That group included five defensive starters and one prominent reserve: Leonard Marshall, LT, Erik Howard, Gary Reasons, Maurice Carthon, and Mark Collins. The latter four agreed to contracts relatively quickly, but Marshall and Taylor took significantly more time.

"I was on the telephone with Bill Parcells every day for three weeks during the holdout," Carthon said. "I thought the way the Giants were negotiating with me was unfair because they kept bringing up my statistics even though I was a blocking fullback who wasn't going to put up a lot of numbers.

"Our tight ends coach Mike Pope would always joke with me that the way I played it was [as] if I played 40 games in a season and went through two training camps. One of the things that motivated me was that we had Pepper Johnson and Mark Bavaro on our team, two of the hardest-working guys...

11

I wanted to earn their respect, because no matter how hard you worked or watched film, Pepper would be in there after you."

Marshall, like Taylor, was playing a lot of golf during the preseason. He considered joining the New Orleans Saints, who had a more exciting 3-4 scheme that would have allowed him to record more sacks. Plus, the thought of playing with Jumpy "the Forklift" Geathers, a 6'7", 290-pound defensive lineman who was known for literally picking up offensive linemen and carrying them back to the quarterback, was appealing. Marshall and the Giants eventually agreed to a three-year $2.6 million deal that gave him $800,000 in 1990, $875,000 in 1991, and $925,000 in 1992. Marshall thought he deserved the $1.2 million that Howie Long earned because his sack numbers compared favorably. (Marshall had 9.5 sacks in 1989 whereas Long had only five.) Even so, the contract made Marshall the fourth-highest-paid player on the Giants and one of the highest-paid players in the NFL.

Phil Simms was the Giants' top earner at $1.4 million, followed by LT at $1.21 million, and Carl Banks at $900,000. Taylor, though, was looking to become a $2 million player—a major stretch in 1990. Joe Montana, the league's top earner, made $4 million annually—though he was coming off two Super Bowl victories and had won four in the last nine years. The only other players in the league earning around $2 million were quarterbacks Jim Kelly and Troy Aikman, the latter of whom benefited from being the No. 1 overall pick in the 1989 draft and received a large rookie signing bonus.

During his holdout, Taylor regularly played golf at Eagle Oaks Golf Club in Farmingdale, New Jersey. He believed that the holdout was beneficial to his mental health. Taylor, who played golf alone, enjoyed having four and a half hours to himself. He preferred the serenity over the frenzy of the two-a-days at training camp. Taylor also knew that he had limited time left in his career and many writers considered him to be on the decline. Myers accurately wrote that "LT was no longer an incredible player, but a good force who didn't dominate over the course of entire games."

After a 40-day holdout and absence from the entire length of training camp, he missed football enough that he instructed his agent Joe Courrege to work out a deal. The two sides were at an impasse; the most the Giants were willing to pay LT was $1.5 million a year, and he wanted $2 million. All summer long, Courrege continued to state that LT was a $2 million player. But the Giants weren't buying the agent's rhetoric.

Giants GM George Young finally challenged Courrege to find a team that would pay Taylor more than $1.5 million. Young gave Courrege an approval letter that allowed him to negotiate with the other 27 teams. Of the 28 teams in the NFL, nearly everyone appeared interested and in the course of three days Courrege heard from about 25 teams. The most serious were the Philadelphia Eagles. For LT, the thought of playing with Reggie White was a dream scenario. Taylor and White were the two best pass-rushers in the league and maybe of all time. White and Taylor, along with Jerome Brown and Clyde Simmons, would probably have given the Eagles the best pass-rush defense in the NFL and made them a serious contender for the Super Bowl.

Eagles GM Harry Gamble seemed serious about wanting LT, but was uncomfortable negotiating with an agent and wanted to make a deal with Young directly. Young, though, refused to negotiate with Gamble unless he knew the Eagles were willing to increase their offer from the Giants' $1.5 million. After all, the last thing he wanted to do was lose LT to the Eagles for less money. The cat-and-mouse game continued for several days. Young thought the Eagles' play was simply to stall negotiations long enough for LT to miss the Giants' opening game against the Eagles. LT became more and more anxious, insisting that he wanted a deal.

"One of the things I respected about Parcells was he never would play this cat-and-mouse game with me," Taylor said. "If I had a problem with him, I would tell him, and if he had a problem with me, he would tell me. We didn't have to go through a whole bunch of words and that led to a good rapport between us. We both shared a similar philosophy on football and we both wanted to win."

13

It was also apparent that LT wanted to remain with the Giants. At first the idea of playing for another team was intriguing, but now it felt odd. On the Tuesday before the Giants' opener, Young drove Courrege to his hotel in New Jersey and had a good feeling that a deal would get done. "You could just tell," Young admitted in the local papers. What was interesting about the remark and the way Young handled negotiations was that he relied largely on intuition. There were no complicated formulas, just an honest assessment of where the market was. Even though Parcells and Young didn't like each other personally, they worked well together because they had a competitive jealousy toward one another, and neither Young nor Parcells was a yes man. Each one thought the other got too much credit, and it motivated them both to work harder.

On Thursday LT, confident that a deal was in place, attended the defensive meetings. Later that afternoon, he was called into Young's office to sign a three-year $7.5 million deal with a $1 million signing bonus and a $1,000,000 loan on a life insurance policy on which he would receive about $400,000 when the policy matured 15 years later. The Giants also had to compensate Donald Trump, owner of the New Jersey Generals of the UFL, who gave LT a futures contract with a signing bonus of roughly $1.5 million. Taylor originally signed with Courrege because of his ability to negotiate deals with long-term payouts. Taylor saw Courrege do it with Cowboys QB Gary Hogeboom and Oilers defensive lineman Ray Childress.

"Young did not want to be the guy to give out the highest contract for a defensive player, so he told members of the press that it was a three-year, $4.5 million deal. He didn't mention the life insurance or the signing bonus," Courrege said.

Courrege spent all summer at the Sheraton Hotel across the street from Giants Stadium and would usually spend about an hour a day negotiating with Young. He realized the only way Young would budge was if Taylor was prepared to sit out the opening game against Philadelphia. It wasn't the type of contract that would get done in July or August.

"It was like slowly biting an apple to get to the end. You would just keep biting and realize that when George said 'it,' it never meant 'it.' I think George really regretted giving me that letter because it allowed me to take the train down to Philadelphia right away. But I caught him in an emotional moment and he had his secretary type it up right away," Courrege remembers.

Throughout the contract negotiations, LT became extremely nervous. In fact, Courrege instructed Ivory Black, a close friend of LT who worked under Courrege, to stay with the player so he would remain calm.

"We really, at times, had to get him away from all the hysteria in New York—of people telling him his agent [was] not doing a good job. They were just trying to create a divide. The key was to get him isolated so he would remain calm," Courrege continued.

LT was now the highest-paid defensive player in the league, and the Giants could focus on their opener. On Friday, the *New York Daily News* ran a large photo with LT and Parcells standing next to each other and smiling. It was clear that Parcells was happy to have his best player back and LT was excited to once again be in the presence of a coach who treated him like the superstar that he was.

"The contract wasn't everything I wanted," said Taylor. "But when does a player get everything he wants? It, though, was a lucrative contract at the time, and provided the means for me to carry on with the rest of my life. I don't think George [Young] was serious about trading me. He was just putting it out there. The possibility, though, of playing with Reggie White in Philadelphia would have been phenomenal."

Beyond the holdouts, the Giants had other matters to attend to before the season started when they lost starting strong safety Adrian White. It left the Giants thin at safety, with second-year player Myron Guyton and Greg Jackson. After the Chicago Bears released Dave Duerson, Parcells knew that he wanted Duerson to bolster their depth in the defensive backfield. Duerson, an excellent special teams player, was a hybrid safety who could play linebacker in passing situations and safety in run situations. Parcells, though, didn't have Duerson's number.

Luckily for the Giants, Director of Media Services Ed Croke was a friend of Ken Valdiserri, who held a similar position with the Chicago Bears. Valdiserri, who was close friends with Duerson as both were Notre Dame alums, was in New York for a Giants preseason game against the Cleveland Browns to interview a radio announcer. Parcells blindly asked Croke if he knew how to contact Duerson and Croke referred him to Valdiserri, who gave him Duerson's number. Before free agency started, teams also would also stash players on IR for future use, not having room for them on the current roster and wanting to prevent them from signing with another team. The Giants put future All-Pro kicker Matt Stover on IR. *Daily News* beat writers Barry Meisel joked with Stover about how injured he was after the announcement.

"He was moving as well as you could move," Meisel said. "I jokingly asked him what leg was hurting and he didn't really know. He said, 'Check the injury report.'"

During training camp, Perry Williams also had to cope with losing his starting spot to Everson Walls, who freely admitted that he didn't sign with the Giants to be a backup. Williams and Collins, who were close friends, had a lot of deep conversations about the situation. Collins was impressed that Williams refused to complain, but instead worked harder.

"Bringing in Walls made Perry a better player," Collins said. "That was one of the early indications that we were a really good team. A lot of guys had egos in our defensive backfield, but they put them aside for the greater good. We quickly realized that we couldn't be stopped when we knew our roles and executed them.

"It was also a very intelligent group. We would discuss certain situations and we felt like we could handle anything because we knew how to talk things out. By the second or third game of the season we knew we were really good and had a chance to accomplish something big that year."

Added Walls, "I think Perry wasn't happy with me being there from the beginning. Even though we sat behind each other in the meeting rooms, we never really got to know each other. Perry, though, was a true professional about the whole thing. He didn't complain and made some huge plays throughout the season. I think we really complemented each other well because he was weakest against the deep pass where I was strongest."

Taylor admitted that the 1990 team was more united than the 1986 team, though not as talented. "We're much closer," Taylor said. "In '86 the offense was the offense and the defense was the defense. That's how everybody hung out. Now, it's a little bit different. Everybody mixes together."

Week 1: Philadelphia Eagles (0–0) at New York Giants (0–0)

Against the Eagles, LT hardly showed any rust—despite having sat out the entire preseason—notching three sacks and a forced fumble. There was little doubt that he'd earned his $96,875 weekly paycheck. The Giants hierarchy could hardly complain either, and Parcells joked that maybe he should have held out from training camp himself.

Giants players like Leonard Marshall thought if they won the game it would prove they could contend for a Super Bowl. A critical defensive stand occurred after the Giants took a 13–10 lead. Players on the sidelines said before they went onto the field, "Now is our time to make the offense's work pay off." On first down, Taylor allowed Eagles running back Anthony Toney just one yard. On the next play, Pepper Johnson stopped Toney after a five-yard pass on second down. Perry Williams broke up Cunningham's pass for Mickey Shuler on third down. Then, Dave Meggett returned the ensuing punt for a touchdown to give the Giants a 20–10 lead. Phil Simms, who missed a chance to widen the lead in the first half when he overthrew wide receiver Odessa Turner in the end zone, hit Mark Ingram for a 41-yard TD pass in the early fourth to widen the Giants' lead to 27–10.

Cunningham responded with an eight-minute touchdown drive that cut the Giants' lead to 10. After a Giants three-and-out, the Eagles quickly moved into Giants territory and kicked a field goal, which made the score 27–20. The Giants controlled the clock until they were forced to punt with 12 seconds left. Worried about a potential Philadelphia block, given the Giants' strange history of blowing fourth-quarter leads to the Eagles over the last two years, Parcells sent Banks and Taylor in to play offensive lineman. Cunningham was able to throw one last Hail Mary, which fell incomplete to the relief of all Giants, particularly linebacker Pepper Johnson. He joked in postgame interviews that if Philadelphia had completed the miracle pass, he would have either retired or demanded a trade to the Eagles.

New York had overcome their nemesis; now they could worry about the rest of the season. Myers wrote the next day that the Giants could be Super Bowl contenders if they got an LT-caliber season from LT.

Week 2: New York Giants (1–0) at Dallas Cowboys (1–0)

Parcells was particularly proud of how his team played against Dallas in Week 2, because of the scorching heat at Texas Stadium. The temperature at game time was around 85 degrees, but it spiked all the way up to 96.

The Giants lost cornerback Mark Collins to a leg injury in the game. But other than giving up a kickoff return for a touchdown in the second quarter, the Giants defense was nearly perfect, making the Cowboys appear like a JV squad that was several years away from competing for a championship. In his postgame interview, Parcells admitted that kicking to Alexander Wright was a mistake—thinking he might fumble, but quickly realizing that Wright was the Cowboys' best threat to score. Aikman was in his second year, coming off a 1–15 season in 1989, and Emmitt Smith was in his rookie year with little offensive help.

Week 3: Miami Dolphins (2–0) at New York Giants (2–0)

Parcells often emphasized the importance of playing well against the easy competition. The Giants defense stayed perfect the next week when they played the Miami Dolphins, as the offense held the ball for over 40 minutes. Dan Marino threw for just 115 yards and had two interceptions. The motto of the Giants defense in 1990 was to make their opponents quit—and the physical pounding they gave the Dolphins stayed true to form. In the game's only sack,

Marshall and Taylor nearly picked up Marino and threw him to the ground. It was the Giants' first regular-season matchup with the Dolphins since 1972 and Marino was, to the Giants, the pretty-boy quarterback from the weaker conference. In the third quarter, Giants leading 10–3, the Dolphins were pinned back to their own 2. Marino completed a pass to Mark Clayton and Myron Guyton immediately drilled him. Clayton fumbled and the Giants recovered. Four plays later, Anderson ran for a one-yard touchdown to make it 17–3.

"Most of us, if not all of us, have never played against [Marino] before," Marshall said. "We really were not that impressed with him and almost determined to show him what Giant football was all about. We were going to hit his ass as hard as we could. We hated those quarterbacks who felt they were too good to get hit, and Marino, we wanted to believe, was in the category."

Parcells, though, wasn't thrilled with his offensive line, yelling at them throughout the game for committing so many holding penalties.

"[The Dolphins are] ready to quit and we give them a holding penalty to let them back in the game," Parcells said in the third quarter. When Simms came to the sideline to discuss a play, Parcells told him, "Tell that undisciplined center [Bart Oates] to get his head out of his ass."

Said Oates, "I wasn't bothered by Parcells yelling at me because there were a lot of times that I got away with a hold and the refs didn't call it. I knew that in any drive you had a limited amount of opportunities and a holding penalty could be a drive killer. Plus, I was always a little scared because I knew if I held too many times they would get someone else to take my position."

Fullback Maurice Carthon admitted that Parcells often treated games against weaker teams like they were more important than divisional contests or even playoff games, because Parcells viewed these games as a test of mental focus. Holding penalties made the head coach very angry.

"Parcells always told his coaches that when you criticize a player, make sure to bring him back up the next day," said Carthon. "He would always emphasize the importance of damage control and I think that is what made Parcells special. Players also really appreciated that he never criticized them in the media or if he did criticize them, he always told them first."

Week 4: Dallas Cowboys (1–2) at New York Giants (3–0)

At home against Dallas, the Giants showed that they were not only a running team, but also one that could throw. Phil Simms threw touchdown passes to Mark Ingram, Bob Mrosko, and Rodney Hampton as New York overwhelmed the Cowboys for the second time in three weeks in a 31–17 victory. Once again, the Giants showed their entitlement toward staying on offense when they controlled the ball for 35:38 seconds behind an offensive line that simply bulldozed opposing defenses. The Giants ran 33 times for 136 yards, 79 by Ottis Anderson, and the Giants did the simple things well, like picking up blitzes, receivers reading their routes, and holding on to the ball.

The Giants started their scoring parade after Steve DeOssie recovered a Cowboys fumble. After three runs and two passes, Simms completed a touchdown pass to Mark Ingram, who ran an out pattern five yards deep into the end zone and barely kept his foot in bounds, as replay would show. The Cowboys realized that they would be unable to run against the New York Giants' vaunted run defense.

Three consecutive completions from Aikman to tight end Jay Novacek advanced the ball to the Giants 7, where the Cowboys offense stalled. After a two-yard run from Emmitt Smith, Aikman tossed an incompletion out of the back of the end zone, and Reyna Thompson made a great open-field tackle against Kelvin Martin to stop him at the 4-yard line. Matt Bahr gave the Giants a 10–3 lead on their next possession.

After a horrible 23-yard punt that gave the Giants the ball on their own 40 in the second quarter, Rodney Hampton broke a 22-yard run on a screen pass and a 23-yard run on a handoff, and backup tight end Mrosko made up for an earlier dropped pass by catching a seven-yard touchdown pass to make it 17–3.

The Giants defense gave up its first touchdown since Week 1 when Smith ran for a four-yard touchdown to make it 17–10. The Giants responded with a 12-play, 75-yard drive, capped off by a 27-yard pass to Hampton, who caught the ball at the 7 between safeties Bill Bates and Vince Albritton, eluded their tackle attempts at the 3, and dove just over the goal line.

With 11:02 to play in the fourth quarter, Parcells decided to test Hostetler to see if he was ready to play. He hadn't told Hostetler that week about the possibility that he might play, but Hostetler rose to the occasion. With the game still in doubt, the QB ran for a touchdown to clinch a Giants victory. Numerous players on the Giants were impressed with Parcells' ability to put the pressure on his backups—particularly his focus on Hostetler. Parcells never wanted his backups to get too comfortable or become rusty.

"He was always testing to you to see if you were ready at any time," Mark Collins said.

Hostetler's 12-yard scramble in the middle of the fourth quarter made it 31–10 and Aikman connected with Novacek again on a seven-yard pass with 1:58 left to close out the scoring. Afterward, Taylor admitted that for the first time in a while, playing the Cowboys was no longer like playing a college team. They actually had to be taken seriously. Taylor, who finished with only one tackle and was credited with an assist on another, thought the Giants looked flat at times and attributed it to their lack of mental focus.

Despite the good news on Hostetler, the Giants' victory came at a price. Carl Banks, who played the whole game, dislocated his wrist and had to wear a soft cast. Jumbo Elliott left the game with a leg injury. (He would go on to miss the next nine or 10 games with a pinched something or other, what the press would refer to as a mysterious leg injury.) Battered, the bye week could not have come at a better time for the Giants. One positive note was Reyna Thompson, the Giants' sixth defensive back, who had played well in place of Mark Collins.

"I am happy [at] the way we have played," Parcells said. "But we have a long way to go."

3.

The Ultimate Gift

HALL OF FAME DALLAS COWBOYS CORNERBACK Mel Renfro jokes that the reason Everson Walls has so many interceptions is because he left receivers open so quarterbacks could throw his way, something Walls, who prides himself on his ability to anticipate, rarely denies. It is an old joke between the shutdown cornerbacks and those corners who earned their reputation by picking off passes. Great cornerbacks, or so the theory goes, will prevent a quarterback from throwing to their side of the field—so they won't have a lot of interceptions.

Walls, who had the timing and hands of a wide receiver, prided himself on his ability to create turnovers. It was the reason the Giants signed him in the first place. Unlike some defensive backs, content with simply breaking up passes, Walls badly wanted to make interceptions. From his rookie year in Dallas, Walls believed what separated the good cornerbacks from the great ones was leaping at the right time to take the ball away from the wide receiver. Anyone could break up a pass, only the great ones made the interception.

With his photographic memory, Walls remembers the plays he didn't make. He has also watched Super Bowl XXV multiple times and almost committed it to memory.

Damn, I should have had that interception, is always his thought when he watches a second-quarter play in Super Bowl XXV in which the ball was tipped several times before Walls caught it out of bounds.

Walls' veteran experience led Belichick to hand him the play-calling duties in the Super Bowl. He was in at safety instead of cornerback, his normal position, because of his ball-hawking skills. Myron Guyton, the Giants' other safety, was in his second year in 1990. Walls considered it an honor, especially because it was something that he had never done before. When he was in Dallas, he only worried about covering the receiver to whom he was assigned. He never thought about the responsibilities of the other players on the field. Given the Bills' no-huddle offense, Walls questioned whether it was the best time to inherit the play-calling duties. But in a way, the no-huddle offense made it easier on Walls because the Bills were generally in the same formation. With a limited amount of time to substitute, the Giants had to limit their defensive calls. Walls called "cover two" (two deep safeties) on almost every play.

The Giants practiced with extra noise and reduced the play clock from the normal 35 seconds to 10. Walls was also responsible for deciding which cornerback or safety to send on a zone blitz. The goal was to confuse the Bills offense about which players were rushing the quarterback and which remained in coverage. Walls decided that Giants cornerback Reyna Thompson should be the extra defensive back to rush the quarterback. Walls wore out Thompson because he sent him on almost every play in the first half. Thompson finally asked Walls, "When are you going to stop calling that damn zone blitz? I'm exhausted."

Throughout the game, Giants defensive coordinator Bill Belichick continued to check in with Walls to see how he was handling the play-calling duties. Belichick told Walls what he saw, and he remained confident. It had taken him 10 years to develop that confidence.

* * *

It was his mother who made him go, a familiar theme early in Everson Walls' life. Walls appreciated his mother's instincts, because they allowed him to get his breaks. Walls had just finished his rookie season in 1981 with the Dallas Cowboys and had little interest in attending a labor convention in Albuquerque, New Mexico. His off-season preference was to play basketball, hang out with his wife, Shreill, or drink with his teammate and new best friend, Ron Springs. Begrudgingly, he attended the convention, still thinking it would be a waste of his time. There, he learned about the NFLPA and the identity conflicts that players have between union and organization.

Walls, an undrafted rookie because of a perceived weakness in speed, was the surprising story of the 1981 season, as he had 11 interceptions. He also got two more in the NFC championship and was named a starter in the Pro Bowl. Even so, at the start of training camp, the Cowboys made Walls few guarantees other than to give him a chance. Cowboys defensive backs coach Gene Stallings berated him in rookie minicamp when he gave up a touchdown and didn't try to tackle the wide receiver. "What's the matter with you, boy? If he beat you, you go chase him. Got that?" the coach asked. Walls had never been spoken to like that before. At first, he looked at Stallings with a sense of shock. Stallings stared back and eventually Walls said, "Yes sir." It was the motivation that Walls needed, as he shut down receivers the rest of the season.

Walls had eight interceptions in the first half of the year. In the second half of the season, he only had three, as quarterbacks didn't want to throw near him. Miami Dolphins coach Don Shula told Walls at the Pro Bowl that quarterbacks and offensive coordinators wanted to test the rookie early on. Once they learned about his great anticipation skills, they didn't throw his way as much.

He covered James Lofton in his first exhibition game, the same player he was responsible for 10 years later in Super Bowl XXV. He was so scared that he played eight yards off the line of scrimmage. Lofton teased him, curling his finger as if to motion that he should come down and play closer. When Perry Williams tipped the ball into Lofton's hands on a long pass in the first quarter against the Bills, it was Walls who chased him down. Lofton still jokes that he got chased down by the slowest guy on the field. Despite his impressive performance, Walls only made $37,500 in his rookie year, a small amount compared to what players make today. It was indicative of the reasons players would strike in the 1982 season, a lack of pay and fairness in contract negotiations.

He remembers the well-dressed and noticeably handsome Franco Harris addressing the convention and being heavily critical of the union, perhaps because of his loyalty to the Rooney family. Tensions were high, as the NFL was on the verge of its first major labor stoppage. Players were complaining about their salaries, about how backups often earned more than starters because contracts were not fully disclosed to the public. Walls remembers that he could not have been more disappointed in Harris that day. He thought, *Why he is selling out? Why he is giving in?* 1982 was also the year that the NFL players went on strike and Walls got his first impression of the late Gene Upshaw, who died in 2008.

He thought that Upshaw meant well, but that his approach was backwards. *You work for the players, you don't coach them,* Walls wanted to tell Upshaw. Players began to resent Upshaw, particularly as he earned more money and their benefits diminished. Upshaw's annual salary of $4.3 million was a tough number to swallow for the many retired players who were uninsured or out of money. Walls remembers his teammates being neglected and felt he had to say something. It was what always got him in trouble.

It's difficult to have a conversation with a retired player and avoid a rant about the lack of disability benefits. Most players agree that their pensions are inadequate—especially when compared to less violent sports like baseball. Players are quick to remind fans that many players only play for one or two years. A player needs to remain for three seasons to qualify for the pension. For every Peyton Manning there are a dozen average offensive linemen who scrape by and suffer a lifetime of pain. NFL players, prone to injury in their careers, also pay extremely elevated insurance premiums.

"Paying for health care can be one of the biggest worries for players and their families," echoes former Cowboys fullback Daryl "Moose" Johnston.

Walls, more mild-mannered than many players on the topic, avoids profanity when describing the plight of fellow retired players. Still, he realizes the difficulty that many teammates face when they leave that locker room. He is still shocked by the stories of Giants wide receiver Mark Ingram and running back Dave Meggett. They were teammates, after all, good-natured guys who you see every day in the locker room. Now, both of them are in prison. Some players have difficulty leaving the cocoon that is the NFL locker room, especially when they face enormous challenges. When Walls was a player, if someone got off course, the player's teammates tried to correct it. Without teammates, many players lack direction and make poor decisions they would not have made as a player.

Today, over dinner, Walls asks the ever-inquisitive writer to hold on for a minute as he says a small prayer. Walls is no "Bible thumper," he says, though he attends church regularly. He offers thanks to God because of what happened to him his senior year in high school. Walls' favorite sport was basketball. Football was a consolation, a way to stay out of trouble. He describes himself as a piece of unmolded clay at the end of high school, a kid who had a lot of anger. He remembers at age 12 being told that he needed to change schools because of integration. He didn't like busing and admits that he hated white people. Everything was different about them, he said, and the last thing that he wanted to do was attend high school in North Dallas where *they* lived. The school he went to was only about 10 percent black, and Walls remembers getting into a lot of fights.

"A lot of people might say the white kids were racist," Walls said. "But I am not going to put it all on them. We were mean and we were angry."

Walls had little direction and no money to go to college. His best bet was to follow his girlfriend and future wife, Shreill, to Grambling State, where her uncle was a defensive line coach. He remembers the long trip in his car with his mother. She, unlike him, knew that a scholarship was his only hope of going to college. After attending spring tryouts, Everson stayed behind, chatting with tight end Mike Moore. His mother spoke with Coach Robinson. He didn't know what they were talking about, but when they finally finished talking, Walls had the team's last scholarship. He never knew what was said in the meeting, but he likes to guess.

He thinks she told the coach about her situation as a single mother who had no money to send her child to college. She promised Robinson that her son would work hard and more than anything needed his direction. To some, Walls exuded confidence—but he didn't have any. If people saw it on the outside, it didn't exist on the inside. He admits that some of his anger might have been interpreted as confidence, but it was more about fear than anything else.

He was scared not knowing what was ahead of him. He also knew how good the competition was at Grambling and remembers future Redskins quarterback Doug Williams throwing passes that zipped over his head. He was playing against some of the best players in the country. It sounds cliché, but he says Williams could throw the ball a mile. In some ways, he says, practice was tougher than the games. It's where he learned how to be humble. He learned the art of anticipation that led him to four Pro Bowls and to become one of the all-time NFL interceptions leaders.

"Anticipation is my thing. It's what I do," might be the inscription on his tombstone.

More than just a great football coach, Robinson was a great teacher, someone who taught his players about the importance of diligence and independence. He told his players to make their footsteps larger than the rest of the crowd, a creed that underscored the importance of charity. Today, Walls has a foundation that helps with diabetes research, as a tribute to his friend and former teammate Ron Springs.

It was also at Grambling that Walls learned the importance of healthy protests—something that helped him years later as a union representative in the 1987 strike. Walls' first protest occurred when the team boycotted practice because of the poor food the team received afterward. "Slop" was the best description. The team worked hard during the day and didn't receive a proper diet at dinner every night.

"We let Coach know that it didn't have to be that way," Walls said. "If we were playing hard, we deserved a good meal." The food improved and the team returned to practice the next day. It was a good lesson on the effectiveness of a healthy protest and the importance of compromising.

Walls also spoke his mind when he saw the Cowboys waive future Hall of Fame offensive tackle Rayfield Wright. Wright had only given up 10 sacks in 13 years and had protected Hall of Fame Dallas quarterback Roger Staubach for years. Walls felt the Cowboys showed a lack of commitment toward Wright once they saw him as used or damaged goods. Walls realized quickly that commitment wasn't a two-way street. You had to be committed to the team, but the team was only committed to you when it needed you.

Then Barnes, an ace special teamer on the Cowboys for many years, agreed to take a backseat to the newly acquired Bill Bates, who was better than he was. The Cowboys told Barnes not to worry—they still needed him, or so they said. Then they cut Barnes before training camp. Walls called it the biggest piece of crap that he had ever seen in his life.

After the 1982 season, many players told Walls that he needed to get his money. Each team was different in its negotiating approach. Dallas president Tex Schramm and chief scout Gil Brandt were particularly difficult, deceiving players like Walls about their earnings in comparison to other players. Originally, the Cowboys offered Walls $80,000 per season—a lot of money, but a figure that was well below the amount top cornerbacks in the league earned.

Walls eventually signed a five-year contract for up to $1.2 million with incentives based upon interceptions and games played. He continued to negotiate from 1983 to 1986 until he finally received the contract he was looking for. It bothered Walls that owners tried to insult their players' intelligence. When Walls learned that 49ers safety Ronnie Lott was earning $100,000 more than he was and management denied it, it angered him more.

Walls felt his salary lagged behind other great players drafted in 1981, like Lott, LT, and Kenny Easley, who also played his position. The Cowboys continued to hold his undrafted status against him. Walls' contract negotiation got him interested in union affairs and he soon became a union representative. He learned about the difficult challenges that Upshaw faced when trying to balance the rights of current players versus the retired players. In the 1987 strike settlement, Upshaw was unable to get benefits for the pre-'59ers, the players who retired before 1959. Many had trouble paying their medical bills. Players who retired in the 1960s also received little pension money. Walls said it was something on their agenda, but it didn't get done.

"You really don't realize that the retired players are getting a raw deal until you get out of the league," Walls says.

Two issues would unite retired players against Upshaw in the coming years: inadequate pensions and disability benefits. As of 2007, only 317 players received benefits of the 1,052 who have applied. That number is even more staggering when you consider there are more than 13,000 living retired players. Most of the 317 receive partial football disability, $40,000 a year, which for many is still inadequate because of the severity of their injuries. Receiving full football disability provides a player with $110,000 annually. Few players have received that level of disability since 1993, because the retirement board's inclination is to provide partial disability.

Walls understands why so many of his comrades were angry with Upshaw, but he also acknowledges how hard Upshaw fought for the current players. Upshaw argued that retired players didn't pay his salary and that it wasn't his job to fight for their benefits in a letter he wrote to former Buffalo Bills offensive linemen Joe DeLamielleure. Upshaw also threatened to break DeLamielleure's neck. Upshaw believed that he was doing the right thing and he passionately resented former players who didn't appreciate him.

"Like I said before, I think one of the biggest reasons players were angry with Upshaw is because of the way he talked to them. He was passionate about his beliefs and they didn't sense that he cared," Walls said. "He didn't identify himself as one of us, he thought we were his players and a lot of guys really resented that."

In 1987 relations between the NFLPA and management had reached their greatest moment of tension. The league was trying to break up the union and prevent them from organizing as Upshaw fought for free agency. The NFLPA filed a lawsuit in federal court claiming that the league failed to act in good faith, more concerned with breaking up the union than making a deal. Upshaw argued the union started the negotiating process on April 20, four months before the collective bargaining agreement expired, yet the owners responded by sending out a memo to "get ready for the scab season."

Owners tried to threaten players to return to work. Tex Schramm sent out a memo to Tony Dorsett, Ed "Too Tall" Jones, Doug Cosbie, and Walls, threatening them to return or risk forfeiting annuity clauses in their contracts. Dorsett and Jones returned, while Cosbie and Walls refused. It was a stand that cost Walls $90,000. He told reporters at the time that he kissed that money good-bye.

The main issue dividing the two sides was free agency. At the time, the team that signed a new player needed to provide hefty compensation to the player's old team. Because of the high demands in signing a player, there was, in effect, no free agency. In fact, only one player had changed teams under that system.

Passions were strong on both sides. Schramm was determined not to give in, telling Upshaw that he refused to let the players have movement. Players were angry as well. Oakland Raiders tight end Todd Christensen told *Sports Illustrated*'s Paul Zimmerman, "I don't know how much better the teams that stayed close during the strike, like the Redskins and the Bears, will be. Needless to say, when a Mike Singletary speaks, he speaks for the Bears, and that's valuable. A team that stuck together through thick and thin, regardless of how much money the players lost, will be better off."

The union went on strike after the second game of the regular season when it failed to reach a deal with the league. Players reluctantly ended the strike 24 days later in what owners considered a major victory. Players, who earned an average salary of $170,000, were now largely unpopular with fans and many admired the NFL's ability to survive the 24-day work stoppage with replacement players, the "scabs" who were crossing the picket line.

In places like Dallas, where the word "union" was almost as bad as saying "Redskins," the players were booed when they returned. Walls joked that despite growing up in Dallas, he never heard the word until he was a player. The NFLPA eventually appealed the decision in the court, which ruled the NFL was not in violation of antitrust laws just because of management's refusal to negotiate with the union. Upshaw decertified the union and, through a long process, the players won a ruling in court that stated that it was unlawful for them to be unable to practice their trade with the highest bidder. By 1993, the league eventually developed a new system of free agency that allowed players to move without compensation.

Players like Walls point to the 1987 strike as a seminal moment in labor relations with the league, as it made Upshaw realize that he had to decertify the union. Achieving free agency was a fight that took almost six years, numerous lawyers, and long hours in court. Walls believes it was an important strike for several reasons. He remembers giving the *Dallas Morning News* the salaries of all the players for the Cowboys. Some players were upset because their privacy was invaded, other were upset because they earned more money than players who were arguably better than they were.

For Walls, knowing how much each player earned was a matter of basic fairness, so players and organizations could negotiate in good faith. Management wanted those numbers to be a secret, so they could get away with paying an arbitrarily low number. The second reason was more subtle. The NFLPA, particularly Gene Upshaw, learned how to advocate for themselves and make the public more sympathetic toward their cause.

"We always got outsmarted by the owners," Walls said. "They always looked liked the good guys and we looked liked the bad guys. I will never forget Gene being a guest on one of those Sunday morning talk shows and holding his own in explaining why the players deserved free agency. It was a big step because we never had such an intelligent spokesman before."

*   *   *

It's those little reminders that make Walls remember his best friend and former Dallas Cowboys teammate Ron Springs. The story—at least part of it—is public now, though Walls never sought out the publicity. ESPN, CBS, and the NFL Network all ran features on how Walls donated his kidney to Springs, describing him as a hero—something Walls thinks is strange. Most people, he thinks, would have done the same in his situation. He also disputes the idea of sacrifice. Walls, after all, is in better shape than most retired players. He runs and lifts weights for hours each day. Sacrifice is when you give up something.

Walls didn't admit to it in his memoirs, or in the interviews he did with high-profile journalists, but he made the donation because of how close Shreill is with Ron's wife, Adriane. "Tighter than sisters," he yells. He says it again for emphasis. "I mean *tighter* than sisters." They would call each other twice a day. If they went to an event together, they would call each other as soon as they got home. There never seemed to be a shortage of things to talk about.

Because Ron's son, NFL cornerback Shawn Springs, was away, the responsibility of taking care of Ron fell to Adriane. Walls admits that he was naïve, not knowing that diabetes could have such debilitating effects. Walls noted that with family, their tragedy becomes your tragedy. And they did everything together. They *were* family. Springs wore No. 24, the number that Walls wore to Dallas. Even their daughters were close.

Walls could see the pain in his wife's eyes as her best friend watched her husband go on a dialysis machine. He needed a machine just to go to the bathroom. It was painful—the young, good-looking star football player she married needed help to work out because the muscular atrophy prevented him from opening his hands all the way. Walls was tired of seeing the pain that Adriane experienced every day. His attitude soon went from one of reaction to proaction. *Let's get something done*, he thought. He couldn't take it anymore. Anger became his best motivation.

It got so bad that Walls had to carry Springs from the car and into a wheel-chair, and help him into the bathroom. Even then, Walls couldn't be there all the time. He had his foundation and a wellness development project that took most of his time and money. He, like other retired players, had failed to save his money. The reasons might have been selfish, but Walls was overwhelmed with his best friend's ordeal.

Springs had waited three years for a kidney transplant. He was on the list, but no matches had been found. Shawn had thought about it, but Ron knew there was a history of diabetes in the family and Ron didn't want his son to have only one healthy kidney if he had to fight the disease as well. His father also wanted his son to focus on football, since he was in the prime of his career. This was Shawn's chance to earn sums of money that his father never could have imagined. Walls decided to get tested. Amazingly, his blood type matched.

"Can you believe that?" Walls said. "Compatible on all levels."

Ron didn't want to believe it. His hopes had been dashed so many times before. First, it was his sister who was supposed to donate, but then she became pregnant. Other family members tried, but most weren't matches. When doctors thought they had found a match with Ron's cousin Chris, it turned out that he also had a poor kidney. Walls realized he might be the last hope.

Springs' career ended in 1986 because of injuries. Wanting to remain strong on the outside, Springs refused to let the disease interfere with his lifestyle. Diabetics should drink alcohol in moderation if at all, but Springs started to drink more—almost as a denial. Walls and Springs were together almost all the time—charity, business, or basketball—but he had not told his friend about his disease for many years.

"[He was] drinking like a bitch," Walls said. "He did it because he was scared."

Springs insisted that the doctor said he could continue to drink. Walls believes the doctor meant an occasional beer or glass of wine, not regular shots of Patron tequila. Springs heard what he wanted to hear and told friends what he wanted them to know.

The story was supposed to have a happy ending—and it did for about a year. Springs' recovery went as planned for a while. He could walk on his own, he started working out, and he no longer needed dialysis.

About a year after the surgery, Ron went for surgery to remove a cyst on his arm. An overdose of anesthesia put him in a comatose state. Because of a pending lawsuit, the details of the case cannot be discussed.

"[To] go through all that Ron went through and then to have a freak thing like that happen is just devastating," Walls said. "I didn't think he would ever face a bigger challenge than his diabetes. But I guess sometimes you just don't get the breaks."

4.

Midseason Survival

IN RECENT SEASONS, THE REDSKINS STRUGGLED to beat the Giants. In fact, the Giants had swept the Redskins in 1988 and 1989. Not surprisingly, in the lead-up to their road game against the Redskins, Redskins coach Joe Gibbs praised the 4–0 Giants. His praise focused on the leadership of Phil Simms, Reyna Thompson's special teams skills, and the unforgettable LT, about whom he said, "Certainly, defensively he's the best single player that I think we have ever faced. As an example, he came into this year without the benefit of training camp and started off with three sacks and tears things up like I have never seen before.

"To insinuate that anybody has found answers for LT, I want to make it very clear for everybody—and I hope you guys print it—the Redskins feel like nobody has ever had an answer. He's probably been the difference in the last four games we've lost. I certainly think he has had as much or more to do with the Giants' success against us than anybody else."

The Giants, though, ignored the praise, choosing to believe that last year might as well have been five years ago. They also knew that playing against rookie quarterback Stan Humphries would be different than playing against Mark Rypien because of the increased mobility at quarterback. Gibbs' ability to work with different quarterbacks drew high praise, though the Redskins struggled to find a consistent quarterback through much of the '80s and early '90s. Joe Theismann got hurt, Doug Williams led them to the Super Bowl but was never the same afterward, Jay Schroeder was mediocre. Joe Gibbs was the only coach in NFL history to win three Super Bowls with three different starting quarter-backs. The Redskins had started the season 3–1 and the matchup in Washington was for first place, as the winner would hold the tiebreaker.

Week 6: New York Giants (4–0) at Washington Redskins (3–1)

Heading into the game, it was expected that the Giants would do more of the same—a power running attack that to this point in the season appeared unstoppable. With Rodney Hampton out with a bad ankle, Ottis Anderson could pound inside and Lewis Tillman, who had more speed, would run out-side. Offensive coordinator Ron Erhardt had effectively mixed two and three tight end formations to keep defenses off-balance.

Defensively, the challenge was to stop the "posse" of Washington's wide receivers in Gary Clark, Ricky Sanders, and Art Monk. The Redskins thought they could exploit the matchup between Clark and Reyna Thompson because of the DB's inexperience. They also needed to worry about veteran possession receiver Art Monk, who had caught one pass in 104 straight games.

In later years, Hall of Fame voters waged a passionate battle over Monk's credentials, those in favor arguing that his unselfishness, longevity, consistency, and downfield blocking made him a deserving candidate. Those who opposed Monk correctly argued that he was rarely the number one or number two con-cern of an opposing defense with the Redskins' superior running game and Clark in the passing game. Joe Gibbs insisted that Monk never asked for the ball and played every position, even lining up at tight end.

Mark Collins says that each receiver posed different challenges. Sanders and Clark were fast and shifty, so a slower cornerback like Collins would have to play Clark bump-and-run to stop him. Collins' goal was to keep his hands on Clark just long enough so he couldn't accelerate into his route. In his rookie year, Collins had to cover Clark in his second start against the Redskins on *Monday Night Football*. Clark caught 11 passes for 241 yards. Parcells told Collins after-ward to study Clark and keep a journal with all his routes. Collins listened, and he covered Clark effectively for the rest of his career. He started using the same technique with other receivers. Unfortunately, Collins missed this matchup with an ankle injury. He could have returned early, but his replacement, Reyna Thompson, had a clause in his contract that if he started three straight games, he earned a $40,000 bonus. So Collins elected out another week.

"I really liked him, so I did that for him when he asked for another week," Collins. "Reyna was one of the smartest people I ever met, and he was the classic case of never judging a book by his cover. He would show up with baggy clothes, in dregs, and you would think he was a street fighter. Then when you sat down and talked to him and he could go deep in conversation about almost any topic, making his points in an intelligent and succinct fashion."

Collins was a character among a team of funny players who hung out together in New York at Joey's, the China Club, or Blue Note after games. They also took in their share of strip clubs on Monday and Tuesday nights. They could go anywhere else. Collins always had food and drinks with other defensive backs on Thursday night. Parcells would tell his players in the preseason that his favorite hangout/drinking spot was Manny's in Moonachie, New Jersey, and his players were not allowed to be there.

"It was just sort of something we did," Collins said. "We would always beg Belichick to come with us, but he turned us down. He promised us, though, that if he made it to the Super Bowl, that he would come out with us."

Players often referred to Bill Belichick as Bill "Bed Check" because he was responsible for enforcing curfew and joked with players about hiding blondes in their hotel closets.

Collins also teased Marshall about the darkness of his skin. When Marshall entered the defensive meetings, Collins imitated the deep voice of legendary NFL Films announcer John Facenda.

"He is as black as night, his skin is dark, and he wears No. 70," Collins would say gravely. All the players started laughing, impressed with Collins' confidence and sense of humor. At the end of the 1986 season, before the NFC

Championship against Washington, Parcells announced that all rookies needed to participate in off-season workout programs. Collins announced that he didn't have to participate because he was a starter.

"That surprised my teammates that a rookie was willing to speak up like that. I think that's kind of where I got my reputation for being cocky," said Collins. "When I was drafted Parcells had a rough edge towards me because I was George [Young]'s guy. He wanted to draft someone else.

"Being that I was from California, he also thought I might be kind of soft. I had to tackle a few running backs in the backfield for him to realize it wasn't that way. He also knew how consistent I was. Whether he liked me or not, I didn't fluctuate up and down. That next year, I was determined to come back in the best shape of my life because I knew if I didn't, I would be in the doghouse for a long time. Parcells would make me a poster child for why rookies should participate in mini-camps."

Collins also had the ideal mentality for a corner. When a wide receiver caught a touchdown pass on him he didn't dwell on it, but simply moved on to the next series.

"If you can't handle the mental part of getting beat then you shouldn't be a corner," Collins said. "A lot of guys become shy and start receding when they give up a touchdown. I didn't. Parcells respected that about me and after the '87 season, my second year, he started to leave me alone."

Other top matchups included Taylor versus left tackle Jim Lachey, who had help from Don Warren and Earnest Byner. Gibbs refused to let Taylor destroy the Redskins' passing game and was unafraid of triple-teaming him if he had to. Nose tackle Erik Howard opposite center Jeff Bostic would be a critical matchup if the Redskins expected to run the ball. Howard would play, though he was listed with a sprained ankle. The injury was at first considered minor, but Howard, as one newspaper article put it, wasn't exactly dancing.

"I'm sure people on the outside seeing that would think, *Ah, it's nothing, just a bruise.* For just 'ankle' in parentheses, the day after it was about the diameter of a softball. It was painful."

Howard—whose quickness in the middle of the Giants defensive line was a major key to the team's success—never saw the benefit of a bye week. When his teammates were off for two days after the Dallas game, Howard was racing rush-hour traffic to get treatments at Giants Stadium at 8:30 in the morning. The treatments, which went on for two hours, had him constantly stepping in and out of ice buckets. Hooked up to an electric stimulating machine, he used a variety of exercise boards to stretch his Achilles' heel and increase his range of motion. Howard was used to this grueling rehab; he hurt his ankle in the previous season against Dallas. Trainers were forced to shave Howard's leg, spray Stickum over it, and wrap it up using plastic tape, almost cutting off the circulation. The most painful part was ripping off the bandage on the exposed skin.

"Miserable was an understatement. One of the tough things that year was, the coaches were not very understanding. It was before free agency so they could cut you in a second and there was little you could do about it. They didn't really have to protect the player like they do now," said Howard. "But the toughest part was on Tuesday when you reviewed the tape and the coaches would ask why you didn't make this or that play and you would think, *Don't they get it? I'm injured.*"

Howard never wanted to be a 3-4 nose tackle, responsible for occupying two blockers in the middle of the field. In college, he could line up wherever he wanted. He begged Parcells throughout his rookie year to trade him to a team that played the 4-3. Parcells refused. At one point, the coach told Howard that almost every team in the league called to ask about acquiring the player, but he refused to trade him.

"It was a big dilemma that I had with myself," said Howard. "I thought, *Should I make a big deal about it and try to get myself traded or should I try to be the best nose tackle I could be?* At first, I tried the former, but then, after realizing that Parcells wasn't going to trade me, I decided on the latter. I always thought of the nose tackle as the guy who just took up a lot of space. In our defense, you weren't going to make a lot of plays because our job was to create gaps for the linebackers.

"We had to block laterally as opposed to vertically, where you could get upfield. One time Belichick outlined a situation in the film room where I had to beat five guys to get to the quarterback. I knew I could beat almost any player one-on-one, but when I beat the center I often had to beat a guard and another guard to get to the quarterback.

"I think one of the tough parts for the linemen in our system was, the linebackers got all the credit even though we were often doing all the dirty work. I don't care what anybody says, guys want to make plays and receive headlines for sacking the quarterback. Everyone one wants to be the hero, and that wasn't going to happen to us in this system, which I think led to some competitive jealousy on our defense."

At one point during Howard's rookie season, defensive line coach Lamar Leachman moved him to defensive end, behind George Martin. When Howard replaced injured nose tackle Jim Burt after the starter was injured in 1986, he realized that he would stay at the position because of how well he played. Howard finally won the job from Burt before the 1989 season after calling Burt and Parcells into a mini-huddle and telling the coach that he was the better player and that he deserved to start. It was hard for Parcells to argue, and later in the preseason he cut Burt.

"I think it was tough for Bill," Howard said. "He loved Burt. Leachman, who might have been the most interesting individual I ever met, however, couldn't stand Jim. He was a thorn in his side. I had to constantly battle with Lamar about my desire to play defensive end. I was somewhat frustrated because I played well at a position where I really didn't want to be. I was kind of like kicking myself."

Against the Redskins, after a week of practicing with 95 decibels of sound running through Giants Stadium, New York demonstrated their ability to win through the air. The volume from the 54,737 fans at RFK Stadium was even louder, but the Giants prevailed, scoring two touchdowns on drives that lasted for three and five plays respectively. Washington was able to shut down the Giants' running attack, which normally could roll over teams' defenses. Simms completed an 80-yard pass to Stephen Baker, a 61-yard pass to Mark Bavaro, and a 63-yard pass to Maurice Carthon.

The Redskins offense, which hadn't committed a turnover all season, turned the ball over four times, including two interceptions caught by safety Greg Jackson. A year earlier, Redskins quarterback Mark Rypien fooled Jackson on a play-action fake to Gerald Riggs and completed a 48-yard touchdown pass to Sanders. This time Jackson stepped in front of Sanders, with the Giants holding a 24–20 lead late in the fourth quarter, to ensure a Giants victory with 1:34 to play. The Redskins offense controlled the ball for 35:28, the most an opponent had the ball against the No. 1–ranked Giants defense. The Skins rushed for 162 yards, almost matching the total number of yards (191) the Giants had given up in their first four games.

The Giants' first big play came after they took over at their own 20. Because of the injury to Jumbo Elliot, Eric Moore was in at left tackle and Bob Kratch replaced Moore at right guard. On third-and-5, Kratch made an illegal motion trying to anticipate the Giants' silent count with a roaring Redskins crowd, moving the Giants back five yards. Soon the crowd was silent as the Giants ran a classic double-cross schoolyard play (one receiver crosses from right to left and the other crosses from left to right). Baker ran from left to right just as Stacy Robinson ran the other way. Cornerbacks Brian Davis and Darrell Green expected the play but collided, leaving both receivers open.

Dave Meggett's underneath block on Redskins linebacker Monte Coleman gave Simms an extra split second to complete his pass to the wide-open Baker. Parcells loved Meggett, always telling running backs they wouldn't play unless they learned how to block and pick up blitzes. Meggett excelled in these two areas. Once Baker caught the ball, he only had to worry about Darrell Green. Of course, Green was the NFL's fastest man, who had famously chased down both Tony Dorsett and Eric Dickerson from behind. During the early to mid-'80s, Dorsett and Dickerson were the league's two fastest running backs, and to quote Jeff Bostic, "Nobody chased down these guys from behind."

Baker managed to get enough space between himself and Green to avoid this fate. The 80-yard touchdown pass was the longest of Phil Simms' career. (Baker, however, had caught an 88-yard touchdown from Jeff Hostetler two years earlier against New Orleans.)

With 6:08 left to play in the first half, Pepper Johnson intercepted a Humphries pass intended for Kelvin Bryant to put the Giants into field goal range. Jeff Hostetler bobbled a low snap from Steve DeOssie, however, and the score stayed at 7–3. To make matters worse, Ottis Anderson then fumbled in Redskins territory to set up a Washington field goal that narrowed the score to 7–6. But two plays later Simms found Mark Bavaro—who hadn't practiced all season with his bad knees—streaking past safety Alvin Walton and hit him for a 61-yard gain.

"Bavaro was like Perry Williams. When you first meet them, you think they are introverts," Collins remembers, "but when you get to know them, you realize they are some of the funniest people you will ever meet."

A few plays later, Anderson ran for a five-yard touchdown to make the score 14–6. The Redskins responded with a trick play as Humphries handed off to Earnest Byner, unfortunately best known for his fumble in the 1987 AFC Championship Game against the Denver Broncos, when he lost the ball as the Browns were about to tie the score late in the fourth quarter. Reyna Thompson left receiver Ricky Sanders alone to help stop the run, and Byner threw an ugly-looking pass that Sanders caught for a touchdown. The Giants led 14–13. On the next drive, the normally stay-at-home blocking fullback or short-yardage option Maurice Carthon ran into the middle of the Redskins' zone, where no one covered him, and turned the catch into a 63-yard gain.

"It was one of the longest plays of my career. When I tell the players that I coach today about it, they still don't believe it. They say 'Maurice ran for 63 yards. Yeah right.' I should pull out the old footage," said Carthon.

"Lawrence [Taylor] still teased me after the game because Darrell Green tackled me at the 5. He said to me, 'Green was able to blitz Simms, check a linebacker, and still run down the field to make the tackle. That's how slow you were, Maurice.'"

Two plays later, Simms found Bavaro on a bootleg in the back of the end zone to make it 21–13 Giants.

Greg Jackson intercepted a pass at the Giants 2, but the Redskins defense held and forced New York to punt from deep in their own territory. In just under seven minutes, the Redskins scored another touchdown on a Gerald Riggs fourth-and-goal run, as the Giants defense barely gave the Redskins in inch. The Giants now led by just one point at 21–20, but the Redskins never got any closer. A muffed punt led to a Matt Bahr field goal to give the Giants a 24–20 victory.

In his postgame press conference, Parcells called the win a very big step, and even repeated the phrase for good measure. Phil Simms admitted that he thought the Redskins controlled the game and he was proud of his team for winning anyway. On the negative side, Carl Banks reaggravated his injury when his wrist became infected by the pins in his cast. He had major surgery on October 16, two days after the Redskins game, and would be out six weeks.

Week 7: Phoenix Cardinals (2–3) at New York Giants (5–0)

The following week was supposed to be the easy game of the two matchups with the Redskins—at home in Giants Stadium. But because of labor issues postponing the start of the baseball season, the NFL season was in turn adjusted because of stadium availability. The reshuffle meant that the Giants would play the Redskins twice in three weeks. The Cardinals had an exciting 3-4 defense and an offense that provided its share of long plays with receivers who could stretch the field. Still, they were sitting at the bottom of the NFC East.

The Giants were excited about getting Collins back. And Collins, in turn, wanted to prove that the secondary wasn't the Giants' weak link. With the additions of Everson Walls and Dave Duerson making the Giants especially tough in passing situations, the secondary soon proved to be a potent weapon. Walls beat out Perry Williams for the second starting cornerback spot, allowing Williams to play in the slot in three-receiver sets. The Giants also used Duerson in sub packages. Responding to criticisms about the secondary, Collins said, "To be honest with you, that's totally bull. Just because we haven't sent any defensive backs to the Pro Bowl…. Last year and the year before we have done pretty dammed good."

Collins thought it was funny that fans only remember the bad plays that a defensive back makes and not the good ones. "Fans come to see defensive backs get beat," Collins said.

If for argument's sake there are 10 plays in a game and a defensive back makes nine of them, fans will only remember the one that was missed. It was a lesson Collins learned well in 1989. After his best season as pro he broke his ankle in overtime of a home playoff game against the Los Angeles Rams. Three plays later, Rams wide receiver Flipper Anderson beat him for a 30-yard touchdown that would end the Giants' season. Collins, despite injury, stayed right with Anderson, but Rams quarterback Jim Everett made a perfect pass that Anderson was able to catch with outstretched arms. Several years later the two of them were on a radio show and Anderson bragged about the catch. It was, after all, his claim to fame. The confident Collins pointedly asked Anderson what he had done since that catch. The answer, according to Collins, wasn't much. Anderson was a good receiver for the Rams who averaged around 40 to 45 catches a season. He was cut after the 1994 season and played with three other teams until he retired in 1997.

"I think this group of safeties and defensive backs were probably the best the Giants ever had because we could all play different positions," said Walls. "And that allowed Belichick to be like a mad scientist—mixing and matching different personnel. Many thought our two young safeties Myron [Guyton] and Greg [Jackson] would be our Achilles' heel, but they played great. Both were really nice, quiet family guys off the field but were ferocious competitors on the field. I have never seen two guys go from Jekyll to Hyde so quickly."

The Giants wanted to return to their ground game, expecting holes in the Cardinals 3-4 defense as they had seen in the previous contest. The Giants had to worry about stopping the run with backup Johnie Cooks, who replaced Carl Banks. Cooks and DeOssie needed to contain Cardinals RB Johnny Johnson.

The Giants were without Phil Simms after he injured his ankle in the first quarter when Ken Harvey came in high on the tackle and Cedric Mack came in low at the same time. The prognosis would be good, but worried about Simms' ability to plant and throw, Parcells sat the QB for the rest of the game.

Hostetler inherited a 7–3 lead, but only led them to a field goal. With 5:38 left to play, the Giants trailed the Cardinals 19–10 after Phoenix safety Tim McDonald intercepted Hostetler at the Giants 25 and they kicked a subsequent field goal.

If the Giants lost, the Monday morning headlines would center on how with Simms the Giants would be undefeated, and how Hostetler was merely a passable backup. So Hostetler quickly led the Giants into Phoenix territory with less than four minutes remaining, under heavy pressure from the Cardinals' blitzing safeties. He found Stephen Baker, the Giants' smallest wide receiver and best deep threat on his signature post route in the back of the end zone for a 38-yard touchdown pass. Baker had single coverage on Arizona corner Lorenzo Lynch; he faked inside and then ran outside for the touchdown.

Matt Bahr's kickoff was good enough for a touchback and Phoenix took the ball at their own 20, with just under three and half minutes left. Johnson made a first down on two running plays, but gained only a yard on the next two plays before the two-minute warning. The Giants were out of timeouts. If Phoenix got a first down, the game was over. They could run out the clock on kneel-downs.

Phoenix quarterback Timm Rosenbach nearly scrambled for a first down, but was stopped two yards short thanks to a two-part tackle from Walls and Myron Guyton. The Cardinals had to punt. The Giants were still alive.

After the punt, New York started at their 29. Hostetler's goal was to get the Giants inside the 30 to give Matt Bahr a chance at a game-winning field goal. His first pass fell incomplete to Baker. Then he hit Ingram for 26 yards over the middle at the Cardinals 45.

A holding penalty moved the Giants to the Cardinals 40. Out of the shotgun, Hostetler fumbled the snap on first down, missed Dave Meggett on his next pass, and then found Lionel Manuel in the middle of the field at the Cardinals 22 with 14 seconds left. Manuel, once a starter, had been reduced to a backup role—partly because of a decline in ability and his excessive partying habits, showing up late to practices and even games. Parcells had reached his breaking point with Manuel, but needed to cope with him just a little longer.

Hostetler needed to spike the ball. He ran up to the line, waiting and waiting some more. Afterward, he claimed it was because he wanted to ensure that Bahr's field goal was the last play of the game. Even if true, it seemed like an explanation formed in hindsight, as all the passionate Giants fans who still remained were probably screaming "spike that f—— ball!"

He had also wanted to make sure that all his players were set. Hostetler finally spiked it with three seconds left. Bahr's kick sailed through the uprights to give the Giants the win and a 6–0 start, their best in franchise history. Mark Collins said that he had a long, one-on-one conversation with God before Bahr's kick. Perhaps AT&T, who was promoting their long-distance rates that season, should have sponsored the call. Bahr leisurely walked back to the locker room with his thumbs up, as Collins was jumping up and down in the locker room screaming, "Yee haw! Yahoo!"

In the locker room after the game, Howard was relieved—or that was the word he used to describe his feelings after he was unable to think of another word. Howard had been in plenty of close games with the outcomes decided in the final two minutes, but the last *20 seconds* was overwhelming.

Hostetler emphatically cited his statistics in that game to anyone who would listen: 5-for-10, one touchdown, and no interceptions. Hostetler had a bit of bad blood with Parcells, who had benched the quarterback in a start against the Saints in 1988, for Jeff Rutledge. Hostetler had reached his breaking point the following week when broadcaster Sam Rosen asked Parcells whether he was concerned about the quarterback's psyche. Parcells described his apathy toward Hostetler's sensitivity level, saying that if he was unhappy with the Giants he could play somewhere else. Parcells was only concerned about what was best for the Giants.

The reviews on Hostetler's first outing were mixed in the New York press. Harvey Araton wrote in the *New York Daily News* that it was ironic that Hostetler, a man of faith, had finally received the opportunity he had been waiting for after praying the night before. He quoted Hostetler as saying, "I always knew this day would come." Araton, like other columnists, noted that Hoss struggled to throw the ball away under pressure, taking several sacks that were unnecessary.

Hostetler completed 11 passes for 180 yards, but at least five of them were on the last two drives. The win also signaled that Matt Bahr was an official part of the team. Bahr, who autographed a book for broadcaster and former coach John Madden with the inscription *journeyman kicker 13 years in the NFL,* signed with the Giants on September 28 after their kicker Raul Allegre was placed on injured reserve with a pulled groin.

The Cleveland Browns had cut Bahr before the start of the season. Parcells made no secret about his general dislike for kickers because he thought the negatives outweighed the positives. Before the Giants signed Bahr, Parcells admitted that the Giants kicking situation was a constant worry, telling reporters that it drove him crazy and kept him up at night. Parcells liked Bahr as much as he could like any kicker because of his feistiness and willingness to make tackles on kickoffs. Bahr, though, was happy to be just one of the guys.

"You're always being tested, whether it's in practice or with practical jokes. Everyone's that way. Everyone tests one another, simply because the team is motivated to win," Bahr said.

Week 8: Washington Redskins (4–2) at New York Giants (6–0)

The following matchup with the Redskins was the last chance a team might have to stop the Giants from winning the NFC East crown. If the Giants won, their greatest competition for home field advantage throughout the playoffs might be the 49ers. The Redskins were 4–2 and a loss would out them three games behind the Giants. The Cowboys were 3–4 and the Eagles and Cardinals were both 2–4 at that point. The Giants were looking for their sixth straight victory over the Redskins and their third straight season sweep.

Giants-Redskins games had historically come down to several plays in the fourth quarter that the Giants would make and the Redskins wouldn't. Two weeks earlier, Sean Landeta's punt took an unlucky bounce and hit Johnny Thomas' leg—and the Giants recovered and scored what turned out to be the game-clinching field goal.

Washington, though, was excited to play the Giants, loving the competition and the familiarity of their divisional rival. Redskins defensive tackle Darryl Grant admitted that despite the Redskins' recent losses, he enjoyed the closeness of the games and trying to overcome their fourth-quarter mistakes. The Redskins had made several changes since their last contest. Thomas, who muffed the punt, had a sore knee and was on injured reserve. Cornerback Brian Davis moved down on the depth chart after falling down on Stephen Baker's long touchdown pass.

The Giants made it clear to LT that he needed to stay within the system and avoid freelancing like he did earlier in his career. At 31, *Daily News* writer Barry Meisel aptly noted that the days of renegade football for LT were over. LT preferred to be a renegade, but sacrificed his fun for the good of the team. "It comes down to sooner or later the renegade type of football leaves and then you're going to play within the system," Taylor admitted.

Parcells continued to remind Taylor that the attention paid to him allowed other players to make plays. Against Washington, a tackle, tight end, and wide receiver helped keep Taylor out of the backfield. Taylor admitted that if he were an offensive coach of a team playing against him or Reggie White, he wouldn't allow either of them to prevail. Taylor aptly noted that despite the talk of his decline, few teams were willing to single team him or run in his direction.

That was true on Sunday, October 28, as the Giants defeated the Redskins 21–10 to advance their record to 7–0. *Daily News* writer Vic Ziegel wrote in his game story that some might think it was too early to compare the '90 team to the '86 team—but everyone was doing it anyway. Perhaps it was because the Giants won the game in spite of themselves. In the second quarter, Taylor ran 40 yards on a fake field goal only to have holder Jeff Hostetler's pass batted away at the last minute. In the third quarter, the Giants allowed the Redskins to score a touchdown on fourth and goal, and a quarter later they failed to convert a fourth down of their own.

The turning point occurred with the Giants leading 14–10 in the fourth quarter. The Redskins had the ball on the Giants 3 after an eight-play drive, with Humphries completing all four of his passes. Humphries' fifth pass should have been a touchdown, but it bounced off Byner's chest and into safety Greg Jackson's arms.

In the first half, Phil Simms completed 13-of-18 passes to nine different receivers, and the Giants had the ball for 11:57, compared to the Redskins' 3:03. In the second half, Simms completed only two passes as the Giants offense struggled. The Giants led 14–3 at the half, but there was little doubt that the Redskins outplayed them in the second.

Humphries had one more opportunity to lead his team on a winning touchdown drive. Everson Walls, though, ended any hope of a Redskins comeback. The former Cowboys player could read a quarterback, anticipate where the ball was going, and jump a receiver's route as well as any corner in the league. Walls knew from the start of the play that Humphries was looking for Art Monk, so he jumped the route and returned the interception for a touchdown, the first of his career. As the clock wound down in the fourth quarter, Taylor asked Bill Parcells if he thought this team could win the Super Bowl. Parcells normally told players to only focus on one game at a time. So when he answered yes to Taylor's question, it said a lot about what Parcells thought of his team.

Taylor must have found Parcells in a loose moment, because he told the media the following day that none of his players were thinking about San Francisco or anything beyond the Giants' next game against Indianapolis.

It was a focus they would need over the final nine games of the regular season.

5.

Disability Headaches

LEONARD MARSHALL STILL JOKES that when he signed with the Giants in 1990, Dave Duerson couldn't run anymore. Marshall refers to Duerson as a good practice player who was excellent on special teams. Duerson, Carl Banks, LT, Everson Walls, and Marshall referred to themselves as the "Over-the-Hill Gang," a group of players at the end of their careers determined to prove they still had something left. Parcells appreciated how players like Duerson made the 1990 squad possibly the most united Giants team during the coach's tenure in New York. He knew how well a veteran group of players could handle the press, easing Parcells' worry about the media's potential to convince players what people on the outside thought was really going on with the team. Perception could become reality. Parcells always told his team to ignore the "outside stuff" and listen to what he said because that is the truth. To his veteran players, this message was clearly understood. Parcells, in turn, gave these players the trust they deserved. The night before the Super Bowl, Banks, Taylor, and Duerson stayed up all night playing cards. Parcells walked by their room, but didn't say anything.

"He had that look in the eyes," Duerson recalls. "The message was clear: *I might not approve what you are doing, but I know you will be ready to play come kickoff.*" The players played whist all night until 7:00 AM, took a nap, and then boarded a bus to the stadium at 2:00 PM.

"You didn't have to worry about those guys," Parcells said.

Parcells understood the difference in mentality between young players and veterans as well as anyone. While the rookies stayed up all night and worried about how they might mess up, the veteran players hardly thought about the game; it was simply the next item on their agenda. They knew they needed to play well, but they didn't quite buy into all the hype that the media created.

Duerson is now often the target of anger among retired players. He has, by many standards, the unenviable task of sitting on the six-person retirement board that decides the level of NFL disability a player receives. The board consists of three NFL executives appointed by the league—Cincinnati Bengals president Katie Blackburn, Tennessee Titans executive vice president Steve Underwood, and Baltimore Ravens president Dick Cass—and three former players—Falcons center Jeff Van Note, Vikings running back Robert Smith, and Duerson.

Many retired players dislike the system because the NFLPA, they argue, appoints players who are more concerned about maintaining their loyalty to the players' union than the overall plight of retired players. One of their best examples is former board member and mega-agent Tom Condon, who was good friends with the late Gene Upshaw. The disability board often receives little attention in the media because the arithmetic is often monotonous—and the politics are overwhelming. Perhaps Yahoo! Sports national writer Jason Cole put it best:

"I think one of the reasons a lot of sportswriters prefer to avoid writing about the CBA or the retired players issue is that football is a diversion for most fans. It is what they do to get away from their everyday problems. They almost don't want to hear about conflict. They want to sit back on the couch and enjoy their football on Sunday. All that other stuff can become white noise to them."

Another difficulty surrounding this issue is the claim by the league that the NFL allocates more money for retired players than any other major sport. Yet the players claim they receive the least amount of benefits among the four major professional sports. Both are true. The NFL fields more players each season than any other sport and therefore has more retired players than any other sport. A Major League Baseball roster is 25 players, an NBA roster is 15 players, and an NHL roster is 23, whereas an NFL roster is 53 players.

"You are simply talking about economies of scale," Duerson says. "It is easier in baseball for players to have better benefits because there are a lot less of them."

Upshaw, resentful of his critics, noted that NFLPA benefits grew from $88 million in 1982 to $1.1 billion under his tenure. Players, on the other side, point out that only 317 players are currently receiving benefits among the 8,000 that are retired—a staggeringly low number when considering how violent the game is.

Brent Boyd is the leader of Dignity After Football, a group uniting retired football players. He argues that the NFLPA's tactics are to deny, delay, and hope you die, pointing out that the disability process takes two years before the board makes a ruling. Duerson says the delay is attributable to the doctors who have their own practices and other responsibilities beyond hearing disability claims.

Players, many of whom have suffered multiple concussions, claim these numbers are fraudulent, that they don't represent the scope of the NFL players who have been rejected by the NFL disability board or those who have failed to receive adequate pension benefits. Boyd went so far as to say the NFL lies about the links between football and concussions, the same way Philip Morris lied about the link between tobacco and cancer. Many, like Boyd, argue that the board should consist of doctors who have prior knowledge of a player's medical history rather than doctors who are paid by the league.

Duerson insists that the medical board does its best given its parameters.

Duerson takes his responsibility seriously. "I tell players this all the time," Duerson says. "I am not going to jail for any one player. ERISA [Employee Retirment Income Security Act] often ties our hands as to how much benefits we can give out. The doctors assign a number to a player's condition, and even if he falls one point below that number, he gets a lower benefit.

"You have a lot of players who took their pensions early and unfortunately don't have money for disability payments. It is sad, but to say that we are purposefully denying players benefits is just false."

Duerson could set the record straight on many of the cases that have been heard in the popular press if he were allowed to speak publicly about an individual case. He thinks that players who "mouth off" about retired players benefits are the same players who never came to the meetings and never bothered to get educated about the CBA.

"Empty tin cans sometimes make the loudest noise," Duerson says.

A big part of the dispute between retired NFL players and the players union centers on whether the doctors from the American Medical Association who determine disability claims can be dispassionate about their judgments when the medical board compensates them. Duerson considers it the most asinine argument that he has ever heard. Doctors, he says, will not violate their Hippocratic oath to deny a player a medical benefit. More important, he insists no quid pro quo exists, that there is no basis to the assertion that doctors need to keep benefit dispensation low in order to keep their jobs.

"I really believe that doctors feel free to make the ruling that they choose is medically most appropriate," Duerson says. "We really don't put any pressure on them and they don't get any extra money for denying a player a benefit.

"Our role is really to make sure that the money the league gives us is invested properly, and we have a fiduciary responsibility to make sure that the players who have been granted disability are the ones actually receiving them. The other unfortunate thing is, I can't talk about these cases because I am a fiduciary, but if I did I could set the record straight."

Duerson adds that the league tries to make the system easily understandable, yet some players never bother to read the material they are given. He points to a second career savings plan available to players and a medical reimbursement plan that some players are unaware of as proof of the ignorance among some retired players.

"My father's worked in the auto plant for years, and believe me when I tell you ex-NFL players get much better benefits than he ever did. Their contributions are often matched on a two-to-one level," he said.

Still, players who retired in the 1960s and 1970s receive pensions that fail to reflect today's cost of living. Former Cowboys defensive tackle and Hall of Famer Bob Lilly played 14 years, from 1961 to 1974, and earns a pension of only $112.50 a month. Lilly admits that his low pension is partially the result of his election to take it early, as he needed to pay his medical bills.

Clark Gaines, who is the assistant executive director of the NFLPA and was Upshaw's right-hand man, says players need to understand the history of how benefits have grown over time.

"I liken it to the situation of someone who just joined a company and has a great idea that he thinks will solve a lot of problems. That person often doesn't understand the history, and why things are the way they are," Gaines says, in a rare interview in his 25 years with the union.

"Players who complain are often the ones born on third base and think they hit a triple. It wasn't always this way, and one of the tough things for the pre-'93 players to realize is that today's players are benefiting from the fruits of their labor."

Unfortunately, the players who retired before 1993 don't receive nearly the same benefits as the players who retired afterward, even though the earlier players were the ones who fighting for the benefits. Players who retire today receive five years of health insurance, after which time a medical savings plan kicks in, contributing $25,000 for every year played.

"I was a player in this league and lost a lot of money when the players went on strike in 1982 and 1987. I don't get anything out of the strike. But I, like so many players, did it because we wanted our sons or best friend's son to play under a better system. Inevitably, in history it is the next generation who see the fruits of their labor," Gaines says.

Gaines is particularly proud of what the union has accomplished: the ability to shop services to the highest bidder, the protection from being cut after injury, and the right to a pension when players retire. It was a struggle, he notes, that took decades to achieve. Gaines also points out that the union stopped the owners from engaging in unfair negotiation tactics, like their refusal to disclose what comparable players made at the same position.

Gaines wants improved benefits for retired players and thinks one day there will be a more just resolution. At 56, he is starting to feel the same aches and pains in his joints that many of his former teammates and opponents feel.

"A lot of players took their pensions early and I am not going to prejudge them for doing that," Gaines said. "Some of them had perfectly legitimate reasons, because they needed to pay their medical bills. The big question is how to fund the issue."

There are three groups the pension fund must support:
1. The players in the league who have vested, but not taken, their pensions.
2. The retired players who have vested but not taken their pensions.
3. The retired players who have vested and taken their pensions.

According to Gaines, the challenge is, if you increase funding in the third area, it could make it difficult for players in the first two categories to get benefits when they request them. Gaines despises what he thinks is political pandering on the issue, as Congress held a hearing in 2007 to discuss disability benefits with Commissioner Roger Goodell, Upshaw, and retired players who were unable to receive disability.

"Much of what happened in 2007 was a dog-and-pony show. It was about throwing stones at the other guy. Not much will be resolved that way," Gaines said. "It is easy when you get in front of a camera to talk about injustice." Emotion, he notes, "will not solve any issue."

Boyd's goal is to address Commissioner Roger Goodell with one voice. Numerous groups have previously tried to address the problem, like Mike Ditka and Jerry Kramer's Gridiron Greats, but delivered little in the way of assistance to retired players.

"Very little money went to retired players in need from Gridiron Greats," said Leonard Marshall. "A lot of the money that was raised got used for administrative costs and a lot of it was mismanaged."

The retired players' inability to deal with disability problems often breeds mistrust and resentment. Numerous players have pointed out that as much as they distrust the NFL and their union, they distrust one another comparably, because of their inability to organize. Boyd has secured several meetings with the commissioner, but feels they have so far been unproductive. In January 2009, Boyd's group held a private meeting with Roger Goodell at the Newport Sports Museum in Newport Beach, California. From Boyd's perspective it was more a PR stunt than anything else, representing everything that is wrong with the current NFL—a league with $7 billion in revenue that is unable to adequately compensate players from past generations.

Boyd resents that Goodell complained about having to fly across the country, even though he has a private jet. Boyd, who lives in Reno, Nevada, spent four days driving to and from meetings in an old truck that had more than 200,000 miles on it.

"He was in bed while I was still driving through Bakersfield," Boyd wrote in an email to other retired players.

According to Boyd, he sent out a survey to the retired players who couldn't be in attendance and asked them what would they say or ask of Goodell if they had to chance to speak with him. Players gave insightful responses, mostly about how to improve the pension system. Goodell stuffed the papers in his bag and defiantly promised that he would never read them. He refused to discuss the issue of pensions, was committed to improving the disability process but did not give any timetable, and with regard to the growing number of retired players without health care, Goodell said that he "will look into it."

Retired players were also caught off-guard by Goodell's supposed lack of knowledge about the pension issue. For instance, he never realized, according to Boyd, that even though it currently takes players three years to vest for a pension, it wasn't always that way. It was four years most recently, and five years before that.

Boyd also alluded to other logistical problems with the meeting—mainly poor acoustics and a lack of order—as players talked over each other, trying to get their own voices heard. The dysfunction symbolizes a larger theme: the lack of unity among retired players.

Boyd was disappointed Commissioner Goodell failed to schedule any more meetings, saying "no more" when asked about future conventions. Boyd summed up his anger quite humorously.

"If another Goodell meeting was announced to be at my next-door neighbor's house, I would rather stay home and watch TV. I learn more from *The King of Queens* reruns."

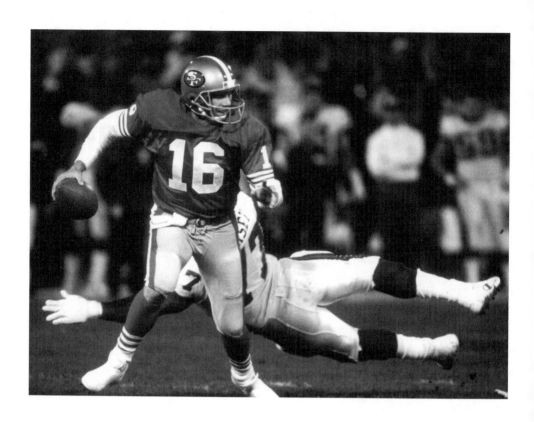

6.

Monday Night Mania

IRONY AND COINCIDENCE SOMETIMES WORK TOGETHER in mysterious ways; the former often explains the latter. When ABC wanted to return from a commercial break with a picture of a full moon, a plane flying into San Francisco International Airport appeared to graze the edge. Of course, it was an optical illusion, but the picture's detail and the size of the plane made it seem like the two were next to each other.

Odd occurrences—like Jerry Rice only catching one pass, for instance—were seemingly destined to happen on this night. Fans and the media had anticipated this matchup for weeks. Both teams were supposed to be 11–0 heading into the contest. Then the Giants lost 31–13 to the Philadelphia Eagles and the 49ers lost at home to the mediocre Los Angeles Rams. Even so, the two teams were still sitting pretty atop the NFL heap.

Week 13: New York Giants (10–1) at San Francisco 49ers (10–1)

Since the start of the 1988 season, the Giants were 1–7 against Philadelphia and San Francisco and 31–4 against the rest of the league. During the 1990 season there were serious discussions about moving the Eagles to the AFC East and the Bills to the NFC East. Other than New York and Los Angeles, the NFC and CBS disproportionately had the bigger television markets in cities like Chicago, Washington, Philadelphia, and San Francisco. The Giants wholeheartedly endorsed the potential move, as the thought of not having to play the Eagles twice a year was an appealing scenario. The Giants, though, loved their rivalry with the 49ers.

For one thing, 49ers nose tackle Jim Burt had been venting his anger toward his former team in the New York press all week. When the 49ers played the Giants in 1989, Burt threatened to angle toward Parcells on a play close to the sidelines. Their feud stemmed from the 1989 season when Parcells told Burt to retire because of an ailing back; Burt felt he deserved to prove that he could still play. Parcells cut him in training camp anyway. Burt, then a backup to San Francisco nose tackle Michael Carter, played well enough that the 49ers put ex-Bill Fred Smerlas on injured reserve with a fake injury, despite a $250,000 signing bonus and $500,000 in salary.

The other main story was whether LT might hit 49ers backup tight end Wesley Walls in retribution for Walls' cut block the year before on *Monday Night Football* that laid up Taylor with a fractured ankle. Parcells wouldn't allow Taylor to injure Walls; that was off limits. But Taylor would find a way to hit him extra hard if he needed to. Walls complained throughout the week that this should not have been a story. He felt the publicity was unwarranted. Taylor himself never called the block dirty, so why were people talking about it?

Taylor complained to the coaches during the week that he was tired of lining up on the right side with Marshall all the time. Even though the alignment worked well, as teams couldn't double-team both players, Taylor wanted the freedom to line up wherever he wanted. When he was confused about a call or the details of a play, Marshall and teammates would tell him to just f—— rush.

"We didn't want him to worry about anything else," Marshall said.

Taylor voiced his displeasure in a speech to a business group at an Italian restaurant in Manhattan. "With Carl out right now, I am used basically as a down lineman and I am basically getting my butt kicked. It's a different type of game now. It's not a game I am happy with. It's making life very difficult now. I'll tell you, I think the way I am being used—I am not saying it's the fault of the coaches, it's something I am not really happy with. So I've lost a lot of my aggressiveness because of that," Taylor said.

Years later, it is a complaint that Taylor doesn't remember. He says now that he wasn't frustrated. Taylor, whose locker was between Harry Carson and Leonard Marshall, credits those two players specifically for keeping him focused on football.

"I was someone who could be distracted easily. Early on, it was Harry, Brad Van Pelt, and Brian Kelley who kept me grounded, but later on it was Marshall. They all did a tremendous job of it," Taylor said.

"It was tough for Leonard," said Walls. "He was a really good player, one of the better defensive lineman I have ever seen, but with LT always being the center of attention Leonard almost never got the credit he deserved and that was probably true for Pepper and Carl as well."

When the NFL Network ranked the greatest 10 pass rushers of all time, LT was No. 3, behind Reggie White and Deacon Jones. Many of the interviewees astutely noted why LT had to be No. 3, as he often lined up against the weakest pass rusher on a particular team. White and Jones were often double-teamed and lined up against the opponent's best offensive lineman.

Many in the New York media thought Taylor, who was about to be named to his 10th Pro Bowl, was no longer the best pass rusher in the league and that he was on the decline. Teammates defended Taylor—particularly fellow outside linebacker Carl Banks—arguing that Taylor was a clutch performer and his decline was simply a media creation. Taylor was asked numerous times how long he would like to play and he jokingly answered that he would play until he was 100 if necessary.

In the ninth meeting between the Giants and 49ers since Parcells took over, 400 writers and 300 photographers received credentials—more than the combined number of credentials issued for the previous year's NFC Championship Game. The 66,092 made up the largest crowd in Candlestick history. When asked whether this was just another game, Giants linebacker Steve DeOssie had perhaps the best response.

"Yeah, and the Pope is just another Catholic," he said with a smile.

Newark Star-Ledger columnist Jerry Izenberg joked that the two teams played and the apocalypse didn't come—though one would have expected it, with about

41 million fans watching. The game drew an overnight rating of 27.0 and a 42 share—that meant about 42 percent of American homes tuned in.

49ers linebacker Matt Millen compared the physicality in the game to what he had seen as a child in the late 1950s and early 1960s, when he watched the Chicago Bears and Detroit Lions play. *New York Post* columnist Steve Serby wrote that this game could have been put into a time capsule and played 40 or 50 years earlier. (The game had all the excitement of an old-fashioned matchup, as it might have put many fans to sleep by the middle of the second quarter. Frank Gifford admitted in the second quarter that if you just tuned in, you hadn't missed much.)

"The Giants knew how to defend our offense as well as any team," said Hall of Fame 49ers safety Ronnie Lott. "So we always knew that playing against them was going to be a defensive struggle. The other thing we would look at was the number of punts our team had. If, by the fourth quarter, we had six or seven punts, we knew we were not doing well and playing the type of game Bill Parcells wanted us to play. He wanted a tight defensive struggle that he could try to win in the fourth quarter."

The Giants held Jerry Rice without a catch in the first half and John Taylor was a nonfactor until the last drive. Belichick wanted to force Montana away from his two favorite targets. Even though the Giants used five defensive backs, Mark Collins often had a one-on-one coverage with Rice. The 49ers eventually moved Rice to the other side so Collins would have to cover Taylor.

"I think it was one of my best games," said Collins.

Before Phil Simms led the Giants on a drive that made it 3–0, the game opened with eight punts and a missed field goal. Simms finally hit Bavaro on a 23-yard pass to open up the passing game and Mark Ingram on third-and-6 for a first down inside the 49ers 20. The Giants only had one turnover, but they just as easily could have finished with four or five. The next play was one that could have gone the other way. Simms' pass deflected off the hands of 49ers safety Dave Waymer—who covered Rodney Hampton perfectly—and into Stephen Baker's arms at the 3.

The Giants' play calling, however, lacked creativity in the two times they went into the red zone. On first down, Anderson ran for no gain. New York tried a play-action pass on second down and Simms overthrew Mark Bavaro. After a timeout, Simms decided to change the pass play to a run at the line of scrimmage; unfortunately, Anderson gained only a half yard, forcing the Giants to settle for a field goal.

The 49ers responded quickly, as Dexter Carter returned the Giants' kick-off to the 37. After gaining four yards on first and second down, Montana called an audible and connected with Roger Craig for a 31-yard gain. Two plays later, Montana hit Taylor in the back of the end zone to give the 49ers a 7–3 lead at halftime. The 49ers gained 63 yards in only five plays, 54 of them coming on just two plays. Gifford said the 49ers offense felt like *tick... tick...tick,* as if it were about to explode. Montana had plenty of time in the pocket—it felt like four seconds on average—but his receivers were rarely open. The game was more of a defensive struggle than most had predicted.

"Our goal with San Francisco was to disrupt the timing of their West Coast offense. That is why Mark would play such tight coverage against Jerry, because he knew that Jerry operated better with space than when someone was right up in his face. Collins and Mike Downs were probably two of the most underrated cornerbacks that I played with," said Walls.

"Mark had a certain bulldog mentality, kind of indicative of his personality. He had a deep voice and walked with a low center of gravity, almost as if he were carrying barrels of steel on his arms. One of the reasons that Belichick brought me in was that I could play both the slot corner and be a safety. So when a team like San Francisco went to a three–wide receiver set, I would slide down and play corner. Otherwise, I would stay back and help," Walls added.

History often ignored the 49ers defense and thought of San Francisco as just a high-flying offense—a finesse team—but their defense was equally good. They had given up only six points in their previous three NFC Championship Games and nothing bothered them more than the "finesse" label. They could hit and hit some more. Jim Burt, Charles Haley, Michael Carter, Kevin Fagan, and Ronnie Lott made up a ferocious group of players who were equally as good against the pass and the run.

The second half had the same monotonous rhythm as the first half. Barry Helton, the 49ers punter—who had the lowest average in the league—punted nine times in the game (and *still* couldn't improve his average). Giants punter Sean Landeta didn't look much better.

There were, however, some wacky plays. One happened when Haley hit Simms, who fumbled, and then Ottis Anderson picked up the ball and ran almost 15 yards across the field to gain just a yard. It might have been the longest one-yard run in NFL history. John Taylor fumbled on a punt return, but instead of picking up the ball he hit it out of bounds, allowing the 49ers to retain possession. On another punt return, Taylor let the ball go for what looked like a touchback. The ball, however, bounced up and stayed at the 1. With just over eight minutes left, the Giants started at their own 25. After a 14-yard first-down completion to Lionel Manuel at midfield, the Giants received their biggest break. 49ers defensive end Kevin Fagan stripped Simms, but Anderson—who was blocking on the play and not looking anywhere but at the player he had his hands on—saw the ball roll right to his feet. He picked it up and ran 20 yards to the 49ers 31. After Simms hit Cross and Carthon to gain 18 yards, Anderson's first-down run set up first and goal from the 9.

On first down, Carter blitzed and forced Simms to throw the ball away. He immediately yelled at his offensive line about who was supposed to block Carter. The 49ers could rush only four or five players and still pressure the quarterback, allowing their defensive backfield to apply blanket coverage on Mark Ingram, Stephen Baker, and Lionel Manuel. On second down, San Francisco defensive back Don Griffin failed to let Ingram create any separation, as Simms' pass sailed out of the end zone. Third down was the Giants' closest chance for a touchdown. When Simms surveyed the field, Bavaro was open. Just as Simms was about to throw, out of the corner of his eye he saw Lott coming, but he threw it anyway.

Lott decked the former Notre Dame star, knocking the ball loose from his hands, and ending the Giants' threat on the lead. Parcells decided that even if Bahr hit the chip-shot field goal, the Giants would have a difficult time regaining possession. The Giants went for it on fourth down, but Darryl Pollard knocked down Simms' pass, which was intended for Lionel Manuel. After the play, Lott got in Simms' face, yelling obscenities, forcing the two players to be separated.

Many questioned Parcells' decision to go for it on fourth down. If the Giants had kicked the field goal, assuming they made it, the score would have been 7–6 with just under four minutes remaining. Considering the 49ers had punted on all but two possessions, it was a curious decision by Parcells—particularly since it was fourth and long. Parcells had to know that the Giants could stop the 49ers offense. The 49ers needed two, maybe three, first downs to win, since the Giants had all three of their timeouts, plus the two-minute warning.

The Giants' decision to throw on all four downs revealed their lack of a short-yardage running attack. Rodney Hampton showed flashes of greatness and an ability to make long runs, but struggled in goal-line situations. Anderson, who passed his career 10,000-yard mark in 1990, lacked the speed and power of his earlier days. The 49ers defensive line also dominated the Giants offensive line, as there were almost no open gaps in which to run. Anderson and Hampton were running right into 49ers defenders. Parcells fittingly wished that Hampton had Anderson's intelligence and that Anderson had Hampton's speed.

"Rodney thought Parcells didn't like him," Carthon said. "But I kept trying to tell him that wasn't true. Parcells was most worried about the rookie becoming overconfident, particularly after he rushed for an [89-]yard touchdown [in the preseason] against Buffalo. He wanted him to stay humble and think he could get better."

Added Parcells, "Rodney turned out to be a pretty good back, but he wasn't better than O.J. [Anderson] in 1990, who was far more consistent and probably did a better job inside. It was tough for us that Rodney got hurt and missed the championship game and Super Bowl."

Parcells also worried that his defense was tired, which was evident on the 49ers' ensuing possession. Roger Craig, on the bench with a leg injury, watched Dexter Carter run for two straight first downs. Adding to the embarrassment, Harry Sydney—a former teacher who was cut by a USFL team!—also ran 12 yards for a first down.

The Giants had one last chance after they forced the 49ers to punt from their own end zone after a three-and-out and two holding penalties. Dave Meggett returned the punt to the 49ers 45 with 36 seconds left. The Giants loved Meggett a little too much when they threw to him in the middle of the field, even though they were out of timeouts. He was tackled at the 49ers 36, and the clock continued to move.

Thinking that Meggett might break one, two, three, or even four tackles, Simms threw to him on the next play as well. He gained another 10 yards, but failed to get out of bounds. Simms eventually spiked the ball with three seconds left. The 49ers, who pressured and battered Simms all night, fittingly sacked him to end the game, even though they only rushed three players.

Lott banged his helmet against Simms' helmet to utter more obscenities. Carter and Bavaro prevented any further melee. Dierdorf probably won the night's sarcasm award when he stated that Lott and Simms were "exchanging words."

"And I don't mean congratulatory words," Dierdorf said.

"Burt was a jokester, but he would always start trouble," Bavaro said.

Perhaps Lott wanted to motivate the Giants if the two teams met in the playoffs.

"We didn't forget that," Marshall said. "We had the feeling we would see them again. Defensively, we could not have played better. Somehow I knew that our offense would find ways to score more points."

Added Bavaro, "Jim Burt had been telling Ronnie all week that Phil said this and that about Ronnie. I don't want to call them lies, but I knew they weren't true. He was good friends with both of them and playing both sides of the coin. In Phil's defense, though, Ronnie probably picked the wrong guy to fight with. He could more than hold his own."

The Giants were 10–2 as they boarded their red-eye flight to Newark. They wouldn't arrive until 6:00 AM. If the season had ended on December 3, the Giants would have been the third seed in the NFC. Instead of having a bye, they would play a first-round playoff game at Giants Stadium. They had the same record as the Bears, but lost the tiebreaker because the Bears had a better conference record.

The players would have Tuesday off, but the coaches wouldn't. They had to prepare the game plan for the Minnesota Vikings.

This game was for more than just playoff positioning and bragging rights. If the Giants won, they would clinch their division.

Jumbo Elliott, the Giants' best offensive lineman, had now missed two months with a severe leg injury. Carl Banks was back after a two-month absence, but played sparingly against the 49ers with a big cast still on his wrist.

Things seemed to be getting harder, not easier.

7.

Life After Football

THINGS CERTAINLY HAVEN'T BEEN EASY for Ben Coates, either. The cautionary tales I'd heard from Duerson and Marshall, among others, motivated me to visit the retired New England Patriot, an All-Pro tight end who played against Marshall. I had heard that Coates was having some problems. For me, the story was all the more powerful as Coates was one of my favorite players growing up in New England. When my friends and I played backyard football on those crisp 50-degree autumn days, I pretended I was Ben Coates—the big bruising tight end who always seemed to make the catch and was impossible to bring down. I was a scrawny child of average height, but nonetheless I made the analogy work for me. It was something to aspire to.

I visited Coates in Charlotte, North Carolina, and what first surprised me was his modest lifestyle.

"The gas costs too much to go from here to Concord, [North Carolina]," was the first thing Coates said to me. By the middle of the 1990s, Ben Coates had made three Pro Bowl appearances with the Patriots and was considered one of the best tight ends in the NFL. Coates did not miss a game in over seven consecutive seasons. He played through concussions, ankle sprains, and back pain. His 96 catches in 1994 set a record for the most catches by a tight end. He was Drew Bledsoe's security blanket—keeping drives alive with his crucial blocks and clutch third-down receptions. At 6'5" and 245 pounds, Coates could outrun linebackers and leap higher than defensive backs. In the mid-1990s, Coates was arguably the best tight end in the NFL.

So when he complained about the price of gas from Charlotte to Concord, North Carolina, it seemed a curious statement from such an esteemed former NFL player.

But to him, "Ben Coates, tight end" is a distant memory. Unless he is coaching or playing he does not even watch football. "You would have to remind me," he says with a smile, referring to his playing days.

During his playing career, he largely kept to himself. *Boston Globe* reporter Kevin Paul Dupont recalls, "Beyond the Greenwood-to-Livingstone-to-Foxborough itinerary, little else has been chronicled about Ben Terrence Coates in his… seasons with the Patriots. Mr. Photo Op he is not. When the beat writers flood the locker room at Foxboro Stadium during the season, he typically slips his way through the horde for an extended tour in the off-limits lunch room. Clever one-liners delivered at his locker? Forget it. He makes a beeline to the buffet table."

Coates refuses to brag about his accolades or reminisce about plays that he made 10 years ago, just as he refused to boast about them then. But get him talking football and he will provide his feelings about a host of issues—the immaturity of young players, health insurance, and the players' union. Today, Coates prefers to spend time with his family and has little contact with his former teammates.

In 1997, when Coates was 28, he received a three-year, $7.5 million contract, including a $3.5 million signing bonus. He played two more seasons with the Patriots but was released in 1999 because of salary cap considerations and declining production. He played another season with the Balitmore Ravens before hanging up his cleats for good.

Most recently tight ends coach for the Cleveland Browns, he has been without a coaching job for almost a year. Coates had spent his childhood laying concrete on roofs with his father and brothers.

"That is what I started doing and I am not ashamed to go back there," Coates said.

Today he lives in a small one-bedroom apartment. The rent is $400 a month. He only has a cell phone, which he rarely picks up, and he doesn't have a home phone.

"Am I lonely?" Coates said. "Hell no. It is peaceful. When I want to relax and watch a movie, I can do it without any of the distractions."

Coates prefers the solace of solitude. He is worried about his many (he prefers not to say how many) children, the cost of health care for his family, and the physical pain he experiences on a daily basis. Athletes have to pay more money for health care because they are predisposed to certain conditions. His own health care bill has exceeded $50,000 a year.

"The money goes quick. With a woman, children, health care, and rehab, it is not endless. For the last year I have been living off my savings," says Coates.

Leaving football also took a toll on his marriage.

"When I was in Cleveland, she didn't want to live with me no more," he said. "She wanted to move back to Charlotte. The money also was not coming in like it once did. You are used to living one style, and then everybody has to make adjustments. It is not easy."

Returning to school or owning a business never interested him, partly because he watched many of his former teammates make poor business decisions. Football is the only profession he has ever known. It is difficult for him to wake up in the fall and watch an NFL game on Sunday. A five-time Pro-Bowler and two-time All-Pro, he is frustrated that he rarely hears from his former coaches. He thinks Ben Coates should know how to coach tight ends as well as anyone. He is worried that his profession might not want him anymore.

"When Parcells took over Miami, I didn't even get a call," Coates said. "It makes you ask why. They call you when they need you, but they often don't need you."

Former teammates and friends can also turn on each other.

"There is a withdrawal effect," Coates said. "Because often you make a deal with a guy when you are playing and he doesn't come through or he steals your money. When you try to sue him, he disappears. I have seen this happen with a couple of guys. You really have to be careful who you hang around with."

"Ben, like so many other guys, didn't get a game plan," Marshall says. "You leave football and you are often not prepared to deal with the real world. These issues often hit you smack in the face. A guy like Ben is not going to get his pension until he is 55. It is about figuring out what you are going to do during that time period."

He spends most of his days with his children, trying to be a good father. "People think I don't have anything to do," Coates said. "There is always something. The kids are always calling me for this or that. There is never a dull moment."

Coates, like so many young athletes, made more money than he ever could have imagined. His rookie contract might seem like small potatoes compared to today's stratospheric salaries, but to a kid from Greenwood, South Carolina, who grew up with eight brothers and sisters, it was a fortune.

"Everything was passed down," Coates remembers. "We did not get a lot of new stuff."

Greenwood was a small town filled with mills and factories. Most high school students worked in the mills after graduating. Another alternative was the military; Coates had two brothers who chose that option. But Coates decided he wanted to play football. He had started playing football in the seventh grade and continued through ninth. He took a break for two years to help his father and returned to football his senior year. Major programs like Ohio State, Michigan, and LSU didn't recruit Coates. Instead, Livingstone College, Savannah State, and South Carolina State were his best possibilities.

When Coates visited Savannah State, his host was Shannon Sharpe. He liked the school, but he realized he might sit on the bench.

Sharpe told him, "Don't come here. You're going to be a freshman and I am going to be a sophomore. They're going to move me to tight end. If you want to play, go somewhere else."

"We still joke about that," Coates says. "There were not enough balls to catch between the two of us."

Coates wanted to stay relatively close to home, but have a chance to play; Livingstone became the natural choice. "It kind of reminded me of my hometown. It was not that big. It was close to a city and a not a whole lot was going on in that area."

Coates was largely considered a steal when he was drafted in the fifth round of the 1991 draft; he would say that the Patriots took a chance on him and it worked out. Coates spent his early years playing on teams that were, to be polite, terrible. 1–15, 2–14, 3–13, 4–12 were the norm. Coaches and ownership changed rapidly, and many questioned whether the Patriots could survive in New England.

"I had so many coaches during those early years, I forget them all," Coates jokes.

Coates spent his first year as a backup, but by 1992 he was ready to be a starter with the Patriots, who were hoping to employ a two tight end set. Coates quickly became known as a film guru inside the Patriots locker room. He spent hours studying tape—anything and everything that he could find. He wanted to understand an opponent's defense to the point where he knew everything by game time on Sunday.

With the arrival of Drew Bledsoe in 1993, Coates finally had a quarterback with whom he was simpatico. A year later, he caught 96 passes and led the Patriots to their first playoff appearance in almost a decade. When the Patriots started the next season 3–6, many local commentators started to question head coach Bill Parcells. But the Patriots won seven straight games and faced the Cleveland Browns in the wild-card round. Coates was matched up against former Giants linebacker Carl Banks.

An older Banks joked about how he defended Coates. Before the game, Banks met with an official and told him that he would jam Coates using a certain technique, something Coates had never seen before. Establishing a good relationship with the official, he went on to hold Coates on every play. Coates started cussing at the officials, while Banks simply praised them.

"As long as you know the zebra's first name, they will give the calls," Banks said.

The story was later the subject of a poll question on an ESPN.com cheating series. "It *was* cheating," Coates said. "And Carl left out one small detail: I still caught six passes for 79 yards. I rarely got shut down."

Coates got hurt in 1995, but still caught 84 passes, an otherwise bright mark in a disappointing 6–10 season. In 1996, Coates helped lead the Patriots to a Super Bowl—catching 62 passes over the regular season. Luckily for the Patriots, the Jacksonville Jaguars beat the AFC favorite Denver Broncos in the divisional round. So the Patriots hosted the Jaguars in the AFC championship instead of having to travel to Denver. The Patriots won that contest and went on to play the Green Bay Packers in the Super Bowl. Coates helped shut down Packers defensive end Reggie White and even caught a touchdown in the game. Unfortunately, the Packers took home the Lombardi Trophy that year.

Bledsoe sung Coates' praises to the media. "He's the best. Until somebody comes along, or his skills diminish significantly, Ben's the best."

Unfortunately for Coates, tragedy was knocking at the door. He learned after the game that his sister had passed away suddenly. He had lost his aunt just two months before. And soon after, Coates found out his mother had an inoperable brain tumor and at 56 she had little time to live.

In training camp the following year, Coates was falsely accused of assaulting the mother of one of his children, to whom he paid $54,000 a year in child support. His mother was still sick, but the judge on the case refused to grant him an exemption. Coates was found not guilty, but his mother died that same day.

On the field, his skills began to diminish. The late Will McDonough, a popular *Boston Globe* columnist, wrote that Coates was over the hill. In 1999, he caught only 32 passes. He played only eight games with the Baltimore Ravens before retiring in 2000 after collecting a Super Bowl ring. He has been trying to find a stable job ever since.

I asked Coates why the money goes so fast. After all, with such huge salaries, players should be set for life.

"You are used to having $250,000 in your bank account every other week. All of a sudden, the direct deposits are only $25,000. It makes you say, 'Wow, I need to slow down,'" Coates says. "I know what I have and don't overspend, but that is not the case with a lot of guys. You try to help them, but what can you do?"

The money, too, can be overwhelming. Cousins whom you have never met want Super Bowl tickets and distant friends ask to borrow money. It seems everyone has an ulterior motive. The money simply creates an environment of distrust.

Coates feared hanging around the wrong crowd. Even Bledsoe, considered a model citizen, was sued—for jumping into a mosh pit at a Boston nightclub in 1997. It was the subject of talk radio for days. One bad decision could easily mean suspension because of the NFL's strict personal conduct policy.

There was also competition among players to see who could have the most extravagant things. If Player A bought a big house, than Player B bought a bigger one. If Player A bought a Mercedes-Benz, than Player B went out and got a Lamborghini. Coates recently sold his Lexus and Mercedes, opting for a Ford Expedition instead.

Many players fail to understand the importance of saving their money and like to show off their newfound wealth with fancy cars and jewelry. Marshall remembers teammates buying their luxury cars right before training camp just to flaunt their money in front of coaches and ownership.

Coates, like so many other retired players, is divorced. The lifestyle change is often too difficult to overcome for many marriages. Often, according to Marshall, money can be the reason for the union to begin with. Players see a beautiful woman, the type who refused them in college, and the woman sees money she never could have imagined. After retirement, a player is always at home, whereas during his career he is always on the road. Normal domestic tensions mount, and when the money runs low, so does morale.

"When the money is gone, the woman is gone," says Coates.

He wants younger players to have a greater appreciation for their retired counterparts whose sacrifice, he argues, has allowed them to earn more lucrative contracts.

"The younger players are getting all the glory that the older players deserve. When you are young, you think the glory is going to last forever. You think you know everything. Everywhere you go, you get endorsements. But at some point that all stops, which is hard to realize when you are playing," Coates said.

It it not so much the money, but his physical ailments that cause him the most difficulty. If he flies on a plane, his elbows are in sharp pain. He is unable to rest his arms on a table without moving them. They are filled with fluid, requiring drainage three times a week. When he sleeps at night, his elbows have to be above his head, otherwise they hurt too much. He points to the table.

"If I were to keep my elbows here for 10 minutes, they would hurt. That is why I am always moving my arms. I played on a lot of hard surfaces, and when your elbow hits the surface time after time, the fluid starts to come into that spot that you hit over and over again. My elbow sac has needed to be taken out."

Coates visits the chiropractor every day. Staying loose is his biggest challenge. He spends his mornings and early afternoons at the gym—running, swimming, and doing Pilates. Afterward, he picks up his children, helps them with homework, and watches them surf the Internet, leaving before his ex-wife gets home.

"You really have to force yourself to get out of bed," Coates says. "It is a lot of things. Some days it is the legs, other days it is the back, which normally hurts the most, and some days it's the feet."

When his children say they want to play football, Coates quickly replies, "'See how I am now? You want to be hobbling around like this in the future?' They see the big posters and they were like, 'You were a professional football player?'

"My kids want to play football and their kids want to play, so the cycle never stops. When my children want to play basketball, I let them play basketball. When they want to play hockey, I let them play hockey—but I don't let them play football."

Coates says that during his playing career he refused to return to a game if his body didn't feel right. But "right" is a feeling, not a medical condition. And in a sport where players get paid per game, sometimes a feeling isn't enough to sacrifice the payday. Coates acknowledges that even in the 1990s concussion awareness was still in its infancy. He often returned to games in one or two plays after a big shake-up. The next morning, the pain was often unbearable.

Coates remembers his worst migraine, which occurred after the Patriots' loss to the Indianapolis Colts in 1995. In the off-season, the migraine returned and lasted for two weeks. Coates argues that while football might have been rougher in the 1970s and 1980s because there were fewer rules to protect offensive players, there is a lot more speed today, and thus more violent collisions.

"You didn't think there would be any harm," Coates says. "But at my age, you really start to feel it. I get migraine headaches and feel dizzy sometimes. The impact of speed hurts a hell of a lot more than it did back in the day. When a 6'5", 300-pound guy who runs a 4.5 hits you, how far do you think you are going to go? Guys used to be 250, 260. 5'5" to 5'8"."

Asked if his physical disabilities affect his ability to find a job today, Coates replies, "I am far from the only retired player without a job. I tell people that the NFL stands for 'Not For Long.' Maybe you squeak 10 years or 15 years in, but when you're done playing your body is going to hurt. It's like two big trucks banging against each other. It's bound to hurt after a while."

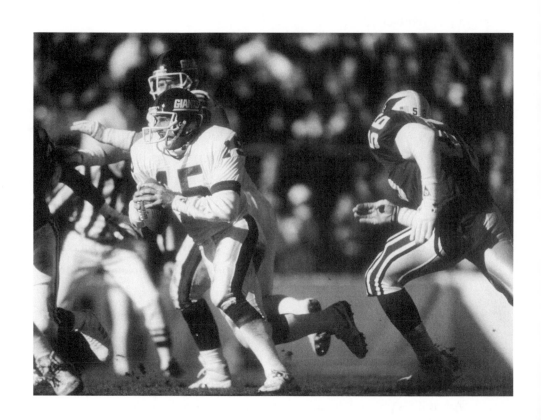

8.

Staggering to the Finish

BILL PARCELLS WARNED HIS TEAM about complacency—telling his players that he needed them today and not three weeks from now. The Giants needed to defeat the Minnesota Vikings to win the NFC East, their first priority at the beginning of the season. Parcells wanted to improve the focus of his players—admitting that coaches must avoid being overly critical of their players after a loss if the team played well. That was the dilemma he faced after the loss to San Francisco—knowing that the Giants and 49ers were evenly matched and the game could have gone either way. Holding the 49ers to only seven points was something to be proud of.

Parcells generated newfound respect among his players because he was battling kidney stones and could have easily taken the week off, turning over the coaching duties to one of his assistants, either defensive coordinator Bill Belichick or offensive coordinator Ron Erhardt. In fact, Parcells had battled this ailment throughout the season. Prior to the Giants' opening game against Philadelphia, Parcells had to pass a kidney stone—just before kickoff. The grind of coaching for eight years in New York was starting to show. Though no one knew it at the time, it was easy to see in hindsight how it could be his last year with New York. He was overweight, having spent far too many nights eating desserts at his favorite New Jersey dining spots.

"For a lot of the season, you could see he was really in a lot of pain," Walls said. "But to his credit he never complained, not wanting to let the players see the pain he was in."

Added Parcells, "I became cognizant that something was wrong after always being fatigued. When I tried to get in shape for the '90 season, it was just something I had a hard time doing. I finally went to the doctor who told me I had the stones. Before the Minnesota game, I couldn't pass this stone naturally, so I went right to the hospital to have it operated on, to move it from the urinary tract back to the kidney. Afterward I went right to work. I think the reason I received them was from my negligence in taking caring of myself. I don't think it was so much diet as I wasn't hydrating myself properly."

Week 14: Minnesota Vikings (6–6) at New York Giants (10–2)

Parcells had little patience after watching his team play an anemic first half against Minnesota. Yet New York trailed only 12–10 thanks to an offense that used a lot of time. Defensive players were upset by the group's lack of energy, the absence of a pass rush, and the inability to get off the field on third down. Linebacker Steve DeOssie called it the Giants' worst half of defensive football of the year. The coaches hardly needed to say anything at halftime, as the players took control.

"We were angry," said Giants linebacker Pepper Johnson.

Taylor told his team at the half, "I am going out there and playing the way defense is supposed to be played. Those who want to come with me can and those who don't, well, that's just fine."

Said Taylor 20 years later, "There are different ways of leading people. Some of the antics I would do during the year weren't like that of a great player, but there was no bull with me. I knew when I had to elevate my teammates' play and attitude so we could stay loose and together. In '86 I didn't know guys on offense, but I started believing that it was good to know the guys next to you and behind you. I used to have a lot of parties at my house to help us grow as a team. I think we became closer as a group. Maybe not as much as I would have liked to, but we did."

"The difference between what I read about LT in the press over the years and the teammate that I knew always amazed me. It was like two different people," said Bavaro. "LT was a quiet, respectful teammate who was always a lot of fun to be around."

Teammates appreciated that Taylor, aside from the antics, backed up his rhetoric. Many who played against Taylor often remember a few signature statements, most notably:

"WE ARE GOING TO GO OUT THERE AND PLAY LIKE A BUNCH OF CRAZED DOGS!"

"I AM GOING TO KICK YOUR F—— ASS."

Taylor played well in the second half. Official statistics gave him 2.5 sacks, but realistically his pressure rarely allowed Vikings quarterback Rich Gannon to set his feet. If QB pressures were counted, LT might have had 10. At the end of the fourth quarter, he made a play indicative of his entire career, a classification best described as "LT manhandles the quarterback."

The Giants led 20–15, and Minnesota was driving. That's when Taylor grabbed Rich Gannon's ankle and forced him to throw an interception to Giants linebacker Gary Reasons, whose return put the Giants inside Vikings territory. The outcome was academic after Matt Bahr hit a field goal to make it 23–15, and the Giants were once again division champions. Parcells told his team how proud he was of them.

"Fellas, we accomplished our first goal," Parcells said.

Week 15: Buffalo Bills (11–2) at New York Giants (11–2)

In the week leading up to the Giants matchup with the Bills, there were continued questions about the Giants' inconsistency. Mainly, a lot of writers wondered whether the Giants could find any sort of a passing game. The Giants were playing "Marty-ball," a reference to legendary coach Marty Schottenheimer's love of running the ball. Wide receiver Stephen Baker joked that even if Jerry Rice was in the Giants offense he would not see a lot of passes. That week the Bills began to assert themselves as an AFC powerhouse, a label that seemed ironic because an AFC team had failed to win a Super Bowl since the 1983 season, when the

Los Angeles Raiders defeated the Washington Redskins 38–9. In the six Super Bowls that followed, the NFC had won by an average margin of victory of 26 points, and only one of the games was remotely close.

Bill Walsh, an analyst on the NBC telecast, admitted that this game would prove whether the Bills were legitimate Super Bowl contenders. Many were skeptical about the Bills because of the AFC's performance in previous Super Bowls. The Bills started to believe their own press clippings.

The "Bickering Bills" had become a common headline. Internal strife and injuries in 1989 led to a disappointing 9–7 finish and a loss to the Browns in the playoffs. The division remained early in the 1990 season when star running back Thurman Thomas was asked about the Bills' biggest problem and he said, "the quarterback." Marv Levy also fined Bruce Smith $500 for criticizing the coach's decision to remove the starters in the middle of the fourth quarter with the Bills trailing 30–7 to the Dolphins in Week 2. Three defensive backs were fined $100 because they refused to leave the field.

Other incidents in 1989 included Jim Kelly blaming tackle Howard Ballard for his hurt shoulder, Thomas criticizing Kelly on national TV, and two assistants—Tom Bresnahan and Nick Nicolau—fighting during a staff meeting. Players Cornelius Bennett and Nate Odomes also left the locker room after their loss to Miami, during the "cooling off" period when the media isn't even allowed in the locker rooms, to find some hot dogs.

"I think we had a lot of older guys who were from rough environments in the south. After the '88 season, we really did a total housecleaning," said Bennett. "But the whole thing about the 'Bickering Bills' was overrated. When Nate and I went to get hot dogs, the stand was right across from our locker room.

"Maybe we should have waited until we put our clothes on. But the media was looking for a good story and so they made that into a big deal. After that incident, we kind of vowed to stay away from the media. We used to hang out at Jim Kelly's house after the game so we didn't have to deal with the bar scene in Buffalo.

"Certainly, there was friction in our offense because we had a lot of talented players that wanted to get the ball. But I don't think it was that different than on other teams.

"We also had a lot of fun. 1990 was before free agency, so it was almost as if we were a bunch of kids playing for the love of the game. Marv [Levy] had a master's in history from Harvard and he would always tell us a story about Genghis Khan or World War I. They often had a similar theme: that 100 warriors somehow beat 1,000 heavily armed fighters."

Owner Ralph Wilson, though, had reached his breaking point over Smith's criticism of his coach, telling his good friend and *Boston Globe* columnist Will McDonough, "I'm not going to put up with this stuff anymore. I'm just not going to stand for it, and I told coach Marv Levy to tell the players that. The next one who shoots their mouth off and disrupts his team will be suspended. And then if they don't like it, we'll get rid of them. I'm sick of all this nonsense."

Wilson seemed unimpressed with the $500 fine. "That's really going to hurt," said Wilson with tremendous sarcasm. "Five hundred dollars to a guy making a million and a half a year should really hurt, sure."

After those comments, the Bills started to mature and showed their onfield ability, worthy of the All-Pro team Buffalo GM Bill Polian had assembled. In 1986 the Bills still held the rights to Jim Kelly, even though he played two years for the Houston Gamblers and they had signed him after the USFL folded. Despite injury, Polian drafted Thomas in the second round of the 1988 draft. When he asked Bills owner Ralph whether Thomas was worth the risk, Wilson's opinion was comforting.

"He said, 'Everything in life is risk. What the heck, do what your gut tells you,'" Polian said. "It was reassuring, though, that our medical staff thought that he could come back from his injury. It made me feel more confident."

Many general managers can pick successfully in the first round; even a causal football fan knows of the best college players. But the challenge is in the later rounds when a general manager must consider myriad factors in determining who can play in the NFL. In the fifth or six rounds, only one or two players might become stars. Finding that player often separates top-notch general managers from the mediocre.

Small schools are often the prime targets in finding such players, as they lack the name recognition of their bigger, Division I counterparts. Some worry about whether players can make the competitive jump from a small school to the NFL. But like anything in sports, evaluating talent is an inexact science—and it was even less scientific in 1985, when teams had fewer scouts and less metrics with which to measure players. Word of mouth and coincidence often played much bigger roles in who a team drafted.

Polian found wide receiver Andre Reed at a small, almost unheard-of school near Allentown, Pennsylvania. When asked about the decision to draft Reed years later, Polian said that he thought Reed could play and that he was particularly impressed with his strong hands and his route running. After all, nothing drives a general manager crazier than a fast receiver who drops a lot of passes and who fails to learn his team's offense. After watching Reed in training camp, Polian was quickly convinced that he had made the right selection.

"It didn't take long to see him in training camp before you knew he was going to be really good," Polian said.

Polian also received tremendous praise for his ability to manipulate his draft board, knowing whether he needed to move up or down to find the players he wanted. A perfect example was his trade for Cornelius Bennett, a pass rusher with blazing speed and an ideal outside linebacker in the Bills' 3-4 defense. Polian orchestrated a three-way trade with the Rams and Colts prior to the trading deadline in 1987.

"I had no idea that I was going to be traded to Buffalo," Bennett said. "I was just a country boy from Alabama who didn't have my driver's license until six months before I was drafted. That's how poor I was. I just wanted to keep playing football. My agent and I kept trying to negotiate with Indianapolis and then they would remove the offer by the time we arrived.

"We went there so many times, thinking we had a deal only to have it snatched away from us. They had the second pick in the draft and I was rated probably as the best player in the country. But they didn't want to pay me like it. When I got to Buffalo, they instantly respected me and paid me what I deserved."

Blockbuster trades in the NFL often work out heavily in favor of one side or the other, and this instance was no different. When the Dallas Cowboys traded Herschel Walker to the Vikings for a bevy of picks in the late 1980s, they drafted players who helped them win three Super Bowls. The Vikings, who thought they were just one player away, were competitive, but they still lacked the firepower to overtake the Giants, 49ers, and Bears. (And a few years later, Dallas was able to re-sign Walker.)

The trade for Bennett was equally lopsided. The Rams, in return for trading All-Pro and future Hall of Fame running back Eric Dickerson, received two No. 1 picks from the Bills in 1988 and 1989, along with Indianapolis' No. 1 pick and three second-round picks. The Rams' picks amounted to mostly mediocre players, yet the Bills had an excellent pass rusher and the Colts received Dickerson, whom many consider to be one of the 10 greatest running backs in NFL history.

"I think Marv and I loved each other early on because I was most concerned about winning and making my teammates better. He is still one of my favorite people in the world today. If he told me that I needed to block the running back, I wasn't going to complain. He knew I did what was asked of me. There were times when I think I could have had 100 sacks and made the Hall of Fame, but I am far happier with what our team achieved collectively today," Cornelius Bennett said.

"It's why, when I fight for the benefits of retired players, I fight collectively. I even want the players who helped us win, but played only one or two years, to receive a pension. There were a lot guys beyond the headlines that helped us win who should receive more credit."

Polian orchestrated other trades for stout middle linebacker Shane Conlan as well as Nate Odomes. He recognized instantly that Kelly was a perfect fit for the no-huddle offense. He had an unbridled confidence and an arm that could throw the ball everywhere on the field. It allowed the Bills to run one of the last true no-huddle offenses (not to be confused with today's hurry-up that teams run in the fourth quarter with time winding down). Kelly chose between five and 10 plays for each defensive alignment and called the play at the line of scrimmage.

By the time the Bills and Giants played in 1990, the Bills defense had finally gelled. Smith, who was drafted with the first pick in 1985, was statistically the best pass rusher in football, thanks to a newfound work ethic and improved attitude, largely through the influence of Darryl Talley. When Talley arrived in Buffalo, Smith regularly ate 100 chicken wings on a night out. Talley never saw so many empty bones in his life.

"Bruce was overweight and difficult to work with when we first drafted him," Bills coach Marv Levy said. "But Darryl really did a great job with him, motivating him to play his best. You really have to give Talley a lot of credit."

Added Bennett, "When Bruce Smith was suspended in 1989, that was really the kick in the butt that he needed. He came into training camp [in 1990] 30 pounds lighter than he was the year before and he evolved into one of the league's best pass rushers. We would always joke with him that even if it was third and inches he would think that it was a pass—ready to start five yards up field and rush the passer."

Talley understood how good Smith could be, particularly if he listened and kept himself in shape. Talley also defended Smith when he made immature statements to the press. In the days before the game, Smith acknowledged that while LT had been the NFL's best pass rusher in the 1980s, he had taken it a notch above. Smith had reason to feel empowered; his sack numbers made fans think of LT. After his rookie year in 1985, in which he only recorded 6.5 sacks, his sack numbers are staggering:

YEAR	SACKS
1986	15.0
1987	12.0
1988	11.0
1989	13.0
1990	19.0

1990 was his best season, but something seemed odd about Smith claiming that he was better than the consensus defensive player of the decade. Someone else was supposed to say it, not him. Talley told the New York media to calm down, that Bruce was just being Bruce, and that he got a little carried away. Talley, however, didn't compare Smith to other players, but described how good he thought he was.

"Bruce was in the best shape of his life. He could throw a 300-pound man a mile, and if three people were blocking him he could still get to the quarterback," Talley said.

Jerry Izenberg appropriately called Talley the "Rodney Dangerfield of outside linebackers" because he was a Pro Bowl-caliber player who had yet to make the Pro Bowl, often overshadowed by Smith and Bennett. Talley was also the player who made a lot of important tackles that failed to show up on the stat sheet. Coming into the matchup with the Giants, he had 93 tackles, four sacks, and two interceptions. Talley complimented the diversity of his defense, telling reporters that the Bills had players who were both nimble on their feet and guys known as "sluggers," players who could get off blocks and make tackles. He called the AFC finesse label a bunch of media nonsense.

For all of the excitement, all of the preamble in what should have been an exciting matchup between Jim Kelly and Phil Simms turned it into a game of keepaway between two backup quarterbacks in Frank Reich and Jeff Hostetler. Kelly had a slight tear in his MCL and would miss the remainder of the regular season. Simms had a severely sprained foot and would miss the rest of the regular season and the playoffs.

Despite muddy and rainy conditions, the game started with a bang. The Giants scored their first and only touchdown of the afternoon on the game's opening drive. They opened with three straight runs from Lewis Tillman, earning the Giants a first down. Smith, though, showed his ability to stop the off-tackle run as he consumed two blockers. Rodney Hampton managed to get by, exploding for a 40-yard run from midfield to the 10. After a Hampton five-yard run to the 5, Giants fans started to show their frustration over the conservative play calling.

On a rollout to the left, Simms had a lane to run for a touchdown. He didn't take it, even though the Bills had no pass rush. He threw a pass that Bills DL Leon Seals batted into the air before Hampton caught it at the 2. Perhaps he was tired from all the pizza he had been eating. Simms had bought over $22,000 worth of pizza in his 12 years (to this point) with the Giants, as he bought about $200 worth of pizza every Friday for his teammates. It was a tradition he inherited from previous Giants quarterbacks.

Fittingly, when Hostetler came in for Simms the Giants crowd gave him a standing ovation after a few successful rollout runs. Hampton ran two more yards to the one-inch line before Anderson plowed his way in for a touchdown. Hampton had rushed for almost 50 yards on the first drive. He would have his best game of the season, as he rushed for more than 100 yards for the first time in his career.

"I was really disappointed in the Giants crowd," Carthon said. "It really hurt me personally to see them boo Phil and then cheer when he got hurt. He was really a great leader for the Giants organization and I never thought Phil got the credit he deserved.

"When I played we didn't have OTAs [organized team activities] and Phil would still work with his receivers and running backs during the off-season. I don't think he is what a lot of fans wanted in a leader. He used to turn down merchandise and commercial opportunities where he could have made a lot of money to focus on football. Even during the off-season, he always left his mornings free for football. In the afternoon, he would do the other stuff.

"He was also so [tuned in] to where we were as an offense. One of our receivers, Odessa Turner, had a stuttering problem and on one particular play he was the substituting wide receiver, so the coaches gave him the play to give to Phil. When Odessa started to stutter we were immediately confused, but Phil knew exactly what play the coaches wanted to run in that situation. He called it and there were no issues. He made you feel comfortable and was definitely the guy you wanted to be in the huddle with."

Said LT, "Phil and I really didn't get along until 1985 or 1986. We didn't have a relationship. When we first won the Super Bowl in 1986, I didn't even know who a lot of the guys on offense were. But over time our team became closer. I developed a pretty good relationship with Phil and I recognized we needed him to win. You need a guy who knows how to win down the stretch. By 1990 we really became a united group and I now think Phil deserves to be in the Hall of Fame."

The Bills' opening drive and the first quarter was the Thurman Thomas show, as the back caught a screen pass for 48 yards to set up the Bills' first touchdown. Thomas showed maturity as he waited for his blockers to be in front of him so he could use his speed in the open field. Thomas had 80 of his 125 all-purpose yards on the Bills' first two drives. Fans probably understood why Barry Sanders was Thomas' backup at Oklahoma State.

Jim Kelly connected with Andre Reed for a six-yard touchdown pass. It was especially frustrating for Bill Belichick, whose first goal was to stop the Bills receivers from coming over the middle. Reed might have given Belichick an aneurism on the Bills' second drive when he caught a pass over the middle that led to a 36-yard gain. Early on, the praise for Kelly couldn't have been higher.

"I don't think I have ever seen Kelly play better," said Walsh, who described Belichick as a bruising, intelligent technician.

The Giants, though, had some opportunities to create turnovers. Mark Collins missed an interception on the Bills' first touchdown drive when Kelly threw a careless pass to James Lofton. And Taylor could have run for an easy touchdown in the second quarter when Kelly left a screen pass in the air for too long.

Despite the missed opportunities, the Giants defense held strong, preventing the Bills offense from doing much of anything in the rest of the game. Belichick realized that using two down linemen was the best strategy to stopping Thomas because it allowed his linebackers to shoot the gaps where they saw fit. It also prevented the Bills' large offensive line from overpowering the Giants' weaker defensive line.

The Giants' passing game, though, remained anemic. Concerns lingered about the Giants' inability to score in goal-line situations. This was particularly acute in the third quarter, when Anderson failed to run for a touchdown because Carthon missed a block, forcing the Giants to settle for a field goal on a 16-play drive that was cobbled together from mostly running plays and Hostetler bootlegs.

Simms hurt his foot earlier in the drive on a similar play to the one on which Kelly hurt himself—a defensive lineman driving an offensive lineman into the quarterback. When Hostetler, standing on the sideline and soaking wet, first saw Simms on the ground, he thought to himself, *Get up. Get up.* He almost didn't want to play, thinking it would be a replay of what happened against Phoenix earlier in the season. He would relieve Simms, lead the Giants to a comeback victory, and then watch Simms return to start. The tease of being a starter was almost worse than not playing at all.

"Jeff was a high-stung kid who was a competitor. And the last thing he wanted to do was sit on the bench. It was no secret why he was upset," said Parcells. "But as a coach, I have to make a decision based on what is right at the time, think about how it will transpire and what the byproduct of that decision will mean for the team. Everyone can't play, even though everyone might want to play."

Hostetler had now been a backup for seven years—2,000 days. It felt like an eternity. Two days before the Giants-Bills game he sat at the kitchen table and told his wife that he was done. His plan, at least in that moment, was to leave New York at the end of the season and find a new career or a new team. Truthfully, Hostetler was acting on emotion more than logic. When he entered the game, he neither realized the severity of Simms' injury, nor the fact that the opportunity he had been waiting for was in front of him. Simms sat angrily on the sideline and tried to give Hostetler advice when the Giants were on defense, but the role reversal was now complete.

"I don't remember seeing Phil around that much after he got hurt, because a lot of times injured players, even if they are as good as Phil, can just melt into the background," said Bavaro.

Late in the fourth quarter, the Giants had third-and-12 at the 13-yard line, but a holding penalty backed them up 10 yards. Then Bart Oates made arguably the worst snap of his career, causing a 19-yard loss and forcing a Giants punt. The Giants got the ball back with 1:04 to play at midfield and Hostetler drove them to the 26. His next four passes, though, fell incomplete.

NBC play-by-play announcer Dick Enberg had mentioned that this matchup might be a Super Bowl preview, but the Super Bowl seemed like the farthest thing from anyone's mind.

Parcells cut receiver Lionel Manuel in the tunnel from the field to the locker room after the game. Manuel had arrived just before kickoff and had been drinking the night before. The Giants cleaned out Manuel's locker and he was not permitted to re-enter the stadium. If he wanted to, the security guards wouldn't have allowed him in.

"Lionel really didn't get cut, he more got fired," said Parcells. "It was as much about his play as his attitude. It was and it wasn't an easy decision for me. He had been a contributor with us since 1984, but once you realized he was no longer going to be a productive member of the team, it was an easier decision. I also want to say I never cut a player to make a statement to the rest of the team, even if it appeared that way. We just had other players who we thought would contribute more."

Said Collins, "Parcells had enough of Manuel. If he didn't think you were following team rules, he would cut right you right away. It reminded me of when we lost the opening Monday night game of the 1987 season to Chicago. Parcells cut corner Elvis Patterson on the plane ride home after he was drinking the night before. I think he got cut over Lake Superior. Lionel told me years later that he regretted some of his decisions because he missed a chance to win a Super Bowl."

The Giants' support among the media and even with former players was waning. Former Giants linebacker and future Hall of Famer Harry Carson thought it was an insult that the 1990 Giants were being compared to the 1986 Giants, the team that won the Super Bowl in convincing fashion after finishing 14–2 in the regular season. Carson called this group a bunch of mutton heads who lacked personality and gleefully stated that the 11–3 Giants couldn't equal the 14–2 mark of the '86 Giants. Marshall said his teammates never worried about Carson's earlier comments since he was no longer part of the team. To the Giants, he was just another bitter ex-player with ulterior motives popping off.

Though Carthon admits, "It was tough to hear that because Harry was one of those legendary figures that towered over the franchise."

Countering that image of a soft, unintelligent team was Jeff Hostetler. He was quiet and reserved, but quickly becoming the very picture of toughness. His former offensive coordinator at West Virginia, Russ Jacques, told the *New York Post* about Hostetler's struggles during his college days. "He took shot after shot," Jacques said. "I have never seen anybody play and get hit from every side, free safety, blitzes, corners, and stunts."

Added Oates, "When Jeff wasn't playing, he really did whatever he could to get on the field, even playing on the punt team, hoping to block some kicks. His ability to stay around all those years when he wasn't playing was impressive."

Giants players were also excited about Hostetler's ability to move around in the pocket, a dimension they lacked with Simms. Defensive players knew about Hostetler's abilities, since he was the scout team quarterback they played against in practice. Each week, the scout team functioned to mimic the upcoming opponent's every move. Hostetler allowed the Giants defense to practice against mobile quarterbacks like Randall Cunningham and Doug Williams. Now starting, Hostetler's mobility allowed agile running back and short-yardage receiver Dave Meggett to become an integral part of the offense. Meggett thrived when a quarterback was scrambling and he could bail him out, avoiding a sack.

"He really did an excellent job of simulating the precision and speed of the mobile quarterbacks that we played against," Marshall said. "We knew that opposing defenses were going to have to chase Jeff, and when they did, he would hurt [them]. He wasn't just standing in the pocket waiting to get hit. The other advantage that I thought we had with Jeff was everyone had a lot of film on Phil [Simms], so they knew exactly what he was going to do in different situations. With Jeff, there really was no playbook."

Other headlines that week centered on the Pro Bowl announcements. The Giants had five players going: Pepper Johnson, Reyna Thompson, Bart Oates, LT, and Sean Landeta. Parcells was most proud of Thompson because he was probably the most underrated special teams player in the league. Parcells believed that Thompson was the best gunner he ever saw because of how quickly he positioned himself to make the tackle on the returner.

The big snub, many thought, was to Mark Collins. Before the Giants played the Bills, top receiver Andre Reed admitted that Collins had become one of the top five cornerbacks in the league. Collins almost always covered the opponent's best receiver and performed admirably—holding Minnesota's Anthony Carter, San Francisco's Jerry Rice, and Buffalo's Andre Reed to few catches and minimal yards.

The Giants, however, had little time to worry about the Pro Bowl selections (and snubs). After Chicago's loss to the Lions on December 16, the Giants only needed to defeat Phoenix, a division opponent, to clinch a first-round bye. Parcells thought earning the first-round bye was critical. It would also give the Giants time to rest and develop some new plays with their new mobile quarterback. Put simply, the Giants needed to pass more. Parcells, a pragmatist, thought coaches should design schemes and playbooks that reflected a team's personnel, not the other way around. He loved to run the ball, but knew the Giants needed some more creativity in their offense if they were going to win in the playoffs.

Parcells started to make slow concessions in the passing game and toward his receivers' subtle complaints that the offense needed to be more dynamic. The always-reserved Stephen Baker said that he wasn't going to complain as long as the Giants were winning. The problem was the Giants had lost three of their last four games after a 10–0 start. Parcells always worried about mental complacency on his team, and given that the Giants were scheduled to play the 5–9 Phoenix Cardinals and the 1–13 Patriots in their last two games, the worrying was more acute.

Week 16: New York Giants (11–3) at Phoenix Cardinals (5–10)

Against Phoenix, any concern about Hostetler turned into worries about the Giants' pass defense, which looked dazed and confused, making even average wide receivers look like Hall of Famers. Roy Green had eight catches for 147 yards and Ernie Jones had four catches for 130 yards.

After Mark Ingram made a full outstretched catch for a touchdown to give the Giants a 17–7 lead, Cardinals QB Timm Rosenbach answered with a 68-yard strike to Ernie Jones to make the score 17–14. Giants safety Dave Duerson praised the coaching of Phoenix.

"They caught us in a couple of situations where they made great calls just perfect for that situation," Duerson said.

The Cardinals had other opportunities, particularly in the third quarter when they missed a field goal and Everson Walls made a key interception to prevent Phoenix from scoring in Giants territory. In the fourth quarter Rosenbach hit Cardinals rookie Ricky Proehl for a 47-yard touchdown pass to make the score 24–21 Giants. Proehl, who later in his career made two game-tying catches in Super Bowls against the Patriots with the St. Louis Rams and the Carolina Panthers, recovered the onside kick after it bounced off Gary Reasons' chest. On third down of the ensuing series, Taylor made an eight-yard sack that eliminated any hopes of a Phoenix comeback, prompting Parcells to say in his postgame comments that he would take his chances with LT any year. Carl Banks batted down Rosenbach's pass on fourth down and the Giants had their playoff bye.

Many New York writers were convinced that the Giants would lose their opening playoff game. *Post* columnist Steve Serby thought the praise of Jeff Hostetler was a cop out, as it distracted from all that went wrong defensively. Serby called the Giants' pass rush "more rumor than fact," writing that the Giants aren't going to the Super Bowl, and it wasn't because of Hostetler. Rather, it was a defense that couldn't stop even the weakest offenses in football. Parcells saw the difficulty of turning around a team that was playing poorly late in the season.

"He told us, 'Don't be that guy that wonders why you got your ass kicked,'" Marshall said.

Parcells told his team that nothing can defeat repeated effort. According to Marshall, it's like anything else in life: you get out of it what you put in to it. Parcells never wanted his team to have regrets because they didn't work as hard as they could have. Prior to the final game of the season against the New England Patriots, Parcells spent Christmas Day watching film to prove that he refused to take the worst team in football lightly. He tried to convince the Giants about the importance of the game against the Patriots. Players joked that Parcells marketed the game as if it were "Super Bowl XXV or Armageddon or something."

Week 17: New York Giants (12–3) at New England Patriots (1–14)
But the players knew that they had solidified their playoff position and that their matchup with the Patriots was inconsequential, making it hard for them

to be motivated. It was already set: the Giants were the No. 2 seed and the 49ers would be the No. 1 seed; both teams would have first-round byes. Players treated the game like it was a preseason contest. During one practice that week, Parcells showed his disgust, walking off the field with the rest of his assistant coaches and leaving the players to practice on their own. The Cardinals and Patriots would refuse to "roll over"—wanting to give the Giants their best shot. For them, the game was anything but inconsequential. The Giants learned that they could lose to anybody if they didn't play well, barely escaping with a 13–10 victory over the Patriots in Foxborough, Massachusetts. The short margin of victory was an embarrassment, no matter how it was framed.

The Patriots were clearly the worst team in football. Gary Myers appropriately noted that the Pats had gone from "just plain bad to thoroughly embarrassing to unbelievably incompetent." The 1–14 Patriots had lost 13 straight and had surrendered a league-high 55 sacks. Even worse, New England was remembered for its off-field activity more than poor on-field play in 1990 when owner Victor Kiam and three players harassed a *Boston Herald* female reporter, Lisa Olson, in the locker room after an early season loss. Commissioner Paul Tagliabue launched an investigation into the matter, which led to heavy fines for the owner and players involved. Myers fittingly called the Patriots an embarrassment to the NFL, writing that they always have been and always will be.

Ironically, the court jester of ESPN's game-day show, Fred Edelstein, made a prediction before the Patriots game that seemed outlandish at the time but turned out to be prescient. He said on television that Parcells would retire at the end of the year, take a year off, and then coach the Patriots. Parcells ended up taking two years off, turning down an opportunity to coach the Tampa Bay Buccaneers before becoming head coach of the Patriots in 1993. Parcells was amused, joking that any news with respect to next year was false and that he was planning to stay with the Giants.

Parcells was proud of the Giants' season-ending total of 13 turnovers, fewest in the NFL, but he gave his team almost no praise after their lackluster performance against the Patriots. He believed it was important to avoid praising a team, even after a win, if they played poorly. Parcells held a team meeting during the bye week and lambasted his players for their lack of effort and focus, telling them he was ashamed. Former Giants lineman George Martin, who was on the Giants' 1986 Super Bowl team, said Parcells helped players see the bigger picture, using the tired cliché of seeing the forest and not the trees.

"The press and the outside people gave me a lot of material to work with. They were calling our team a bunch of Neanderthals because our offense was slow and we primarily relied on our defense. They also kept giving these statistics that no team had ever won anything with a backup QB," said Parcells.

"I knew we were 13–3 and had a pretty good team. But the last six weeks of the season we had kind of gone along in a piecemeal fashion. I wanted to change that. I wasn't so much worried about our defense, because I knew how good it was, and we had a lot of veteran leaders. As coaches, though, we had to figure out what we could and couldn't do with Jeff, and eventually we did and were able to rally around him in the playoffs."

Added Bavaro, "We were a boring team offensively. We weren't exactly the team that everyone sat down and looked forward to watching every week."

As a response to Parcells' verbal tirade, the Giants held a players-only meeting in which Taylor, Carl Banks, Mark Collins, Maurice Carthon, and Marshall spoke.

"It was really a meeting where we aired our frustrations with the coaches and with ourselves," Marshall said. "I think what made the meeting successful was we all respected each other. It wasn't the usual locker room, with guys trying to talk over each other. I would wait for the opportune time to say something and teammates would remember it. The same was true for the other guys that spoke. We came out of the meeting feeling united and ready to go."

Added Collins, "When it comes to psychology, Parcells really knows what he is doing. He knew we had a group of veteran players that would turn this dispute into a players-versus-coaches issue and that is exactly what he wanted.

We came out of that meeting determined to show the coaches that they were wrong."

Said Carthon, "Against New England, we really did everything that the coaches told us not to do by taking them lightly and not preparing as hard as we could. We just had to refocus. It was also a gut-check time for our offense because we knew that our defense was our strength, but we needed to play better."

Years later, Parcells admitted he was proud of the 1990 team because of how well his players handled internal conflict. "They handled a lot of the stuff we threw at them as well as any team I have ever coached," Parcells said.

By the time the playoffs rolled around, his players were experts.

9.

Slobberknocker at the Meadowlands

THE TERM WAS "SLOBBERKNOCKER," at least that's how Chicago Bears nose tackle and future Hall of Famer Dan Hampton referred to the divisional play-off matchup between the Bears and Giants. The journey from Chicago to New York was a sentimental one for Hampton, who was, as it turned out, playing in his last game. Hampton, who had six knee operations during his career, was less than excited about playing on the Astroturf at the Meadowlands. He likened it to going to the dentist: something you had to do, but really didn't want to.

Tired of the cliché "smashmouth football," CBS's lead broadcast team of John Madden and Pat Summerall decided to use slobberknockers instead. It was no secret that this game was about running and defense. Fittingly, CBS opened its telecast with Sam Huff, Sid Luckman, and Alex Webster talking about the 1963 NFC Championship Game between the Giants and Bears, which had been played at Wrigley Field in Chicago.

The teams had plenty of rivalry to coast on. There was also the infamous "Sneakers Game" in 1934, when the Giants came back to beat the Bears despite muddy weather. Giants equipment manager Abe Cohen had borrowed sneakers from Manhattan College and the Giants started wearing them in the third quarter instead of their cleats to get a more solid footing. The Giants were excited about playing Chicago partly because Bill Parcells wanted to return to the old rivalry that dated back to the days of leather helmets and $5,000-a-year contracts.

At an NFL owners meeting a few years earlier, Parcells and Mike Ditka had talked about renewing the rivalry as the two were in the steam room together—

exquisite imagery to say the least. With three divisions in the NFC, the Giants and Bears no longer played as much as they used to. In fact, in Parcells' eight years with the Giants, this game would be only the third meeting between the teams, the second in the postseason.

The Giants had lost to the 15–1 Bears 21–0 in the 1985 playoffs, and Chicago shuffled on to win their first Super Bowl. The '85 Bears, probably the greatest individual team of the decade, had what many call the best defense in NFL history and a well-balanced offense that featured Hall of Fame running back Walter Payton. Their average margin of victory in the regular season and playoffs was 19 points, and their defense held four shutouts, including two in playoffs.

The last time these two teams played was the first *Monday Night Football* game of the 1987 season, when Chicago QB Mike Tomczak had perhaps his best game as a pro, and the Bears routed the Giants 34–19. Tomczak completed 20 passes for 292 yards, including a 56-yard touchdown pass to Willie Gault. All told, the Giants hadn't beat the Bears since 1969, when Richard Nixon was in his first term as president, Parcells was an assistant coach at West Point, and running back Rodney Hampton was six months old.

The Bears defense was far worse in 1990 than it was in 1985, but many of the names still remained the same. They still had William "Refrigerator" Perry, Hampton, and Richard Dent inside, with Mike Singletary at linebacker, but their production had discernibly declined. Perry was now 28, Dent 30, Hampton 33, and Singletary 32. Many thought Hampton should have retired a year earlier, but with a 6–10 finish in 1989, he felt odd leaving a team he helped build in the lurch. The Bears rebounded in 1990, finishing 11–5 and winning their division. Drafted in 1989, Trace Armstrong finished with 10 sacks in 1990 and was a strong addition to the Bears defensive line.

Mike Ditka jokingly showed the Bears game plan to his 17-month-old granddaughter Lauren before the Bears departed Chicago. He teased that anybody could learn the game plan because it was so easy. He told her that it was "run straight up the middle, run to the left, and run to the right."

But nothing was that simple. Neal Anderson, the Bears' All-Pro running back, had cracked ribs, admitting to CBS sideline correspondent Pat O'Brien that it hurt to do anything, even breathe. Anderson, though, said he could play with almost any ailment, even without a helmet. Asked how LT might treat him with the bruised ribs, Anderson responded that he would deliver a few shots of his own. LT said he specialized in punishing running backs with bruised ribs.

Bill Parcells, eerily superstitious, wore the same pair of pants with a broken zipper that he had worn for years. Because he couldn't use the zipper, he wore a long coat so fans couldn't see that his fly was down. Parcells also had his collection of small elephants in his office pointed in a certain direction. They were his good-luck charms, telling Madden that he loved winning elephants.

Parcells was concerned about whether the bye week helped or hurt the Giants. Surely the extra rest was beneficial. But Carthon spoke for numerous players when he complained that the time between games felt like an eternity. Parcells' worries dissipated after he watched Friday's practice, when saw how much fun his team was having. Despite wet weather and high winds, players were slipping and sliding around as if they were teenagers playing backyard football at recess. They had their confidence up.

Both injured quarterbacks, Harbaugh and Phil Simms, joined the CBS pregame show and discussed how difficult it was to be sitting on the sidelines. Simms, particularly distraught, admitted that the playoffs were his biggest motivation at this point in his career. Simms, though, hoped his coaches listened to QB Jeff Hostetler when he told them earlier in the week that he preferred the normal playbook and wasn't afraid to throw. Hostetler was tired of all the rollouts the coaching staff called in the last two regular-season games, almost having to convince them that his first choice was to throw and not run on a passing play.

The other big change the Giants made was to switch from a 3-4 to a 4-3 for the first time all year. Defensive coordinator Bill Belichick decided on the change after watching the Bears' home playoff game against the New Orleans Saints in the previous week. The 3-4 defense that the Giants played was more aptly suited to stop outside runs off-tackle than inside runs. With Anderson and Brad Muster, the Bears liked to run *inside,* so having four down linemen would be more effective. The Giants started Leonard Marshall, John Washington, Erik Howard, and added Mike Fox, a bruising rookie defensive lineman who generally played on third downs.

"If a frog had wings, it wouldn't bump his ass when it lands," Parcells told his defense in an attempt to make them realize that the Bears were just a running team. It was a deviation of Parcells' infamous quote "you are what you are" when a team would attempt to argue that they were better than their record. The analogy, though, and the science could have used some work. Still, the players got the picture.

Belichick played the percentages—probably as well as any coach in the NFL—knowing that if the Giants' opponent successfully converted between only 15 and 20 percent on third down, the Giants would win. Belichick often kept his defenses simple on first and second down, but on third down his calls became more varied, with an array of coverages designed to confuse opponents.

By 1990, Belichick was an up-and-coming star. He was the marquee coordinator a team needed to consider if they were looking for a head coach. In the previous year, Belichick was a finalist for the job in Phoenix, which he lost out to Joe Bugel. He illuminated his unique philosophy in a *New York Post* feature that was one of the first to refer to him as a genius. He said that the three statistics he worried about, in order, were: the number of points a team gave up, his team's percentage on third-down conversions, and the number of yards his defense gave up. While the first one was obvious, the next two are noteworthy. Belichick rarely worried about giving up a lot of yards. He was more concerned if his team could get off the field on third down. If his defense gave up eight or nine yards on first and second down but made the stop on third down, he was satisfied.

LT was often the cause of friction between Parcells and Belichick because Parcells believed that, to some extent, stars should be granted special privileges, since they are the players who ultimately allow you to win on Sunday and ultimately keep your own job. Belichick, on the other hand, had a more egalitarian approach, believing players should be treated equally. As the season progressed, Taylor became increasingly focused, especially with his attention to detail, almost never goofing off in defensive meetings with Belichick.

"It was just something he knew not to do," Walls said.

Taylor was impressed with Belichick's knowledge, saying that for someone who never played football, he knew quite a lot. Taylor was also enamored with Belichick's football IQ, particularly his mastery of situational football. Walls also thought Belichick knew the other team's play before they ran it. (Of course, after the Patriots were caught stealing the other team's defensive signals in 2007, Walls sometimes jokingly wonders if Belichick had extra advantages all along.)

The game-time temperature was 32 degrees, surprisingly high for early January. The winds were so strong that Giants cornerback Perry Williams had to hold the ball on the tee for opening kickoff. On the first play from scrimmage the Giants showed their standard defense with four defensive linemen and two linebackers (Carl Banks and LT) at the line of scrimmage. Pepper Johnson and safety Greg Jackson were set where the linebackers normally were. Anderson ran up the middle for one yard on first down. Taking advantage of the single coverage on the outside, Tomczak hit Bears WR Wendell Davis for a 35-yard gain. Predictably, the Bears ran again on first down for several yards. Surprisingly, the Bears were unwilling to throw on first down to confuse the Giants. On second down, Taylor hit Tomczak and Everson Walls knocked the ball away from WR Ron Morris. Tomczak overthrew Muster with Dave Duerson in coverage on third down, forcing a Bears punt.

The Giants departed from their normal offense on their opening play. Normally, Parcells liked to run on first down, but against a strong defense like the Bears, first down was the best time to throw. Unfortunately, the pass fell incomplete. Running back Ottis Anderson ran straight into Perry on second down and Hostetler was sacked on third down, warranting a Giants punt.

Mark Collins made the game's first big play on the Bears' second possession, intercepting Tomczak's pass, which bounced off the hands of WR Dennis Gentry at midfield. On the resulting possession, a Matt Bahr field goal gave the Giants a 3–0 lead.

After Chicago's Johnnie Bailey returned the ensuing kickoff to midfield, the Bears completed a pass to Ron Morris inside the 30. Two plays later, Taylor tackled Anderson for a seven-yard loss and the Bears failed to convert on fourth-and-long with a screen pass that gained only several yards. It was clear that the Bears offense could move the ball into Giants territory, but the Giants did as Belichick asked, holding them on almost every crucial third and fourth down. On the next drive, Hostetler completed a fourth-and-1 pass to backup tight end Bob Mrosko at the Bears 21, then hit Stephen Baker on a corner route in the back of the end zone to give the Giants a 10–0 lead.

Later in the second quarter, Steve McMichael forced a fumble when he hit Hostetler and the Bears recovered at the Giants 38. Several plays later, Tomczak completed a 20-yard pass to tight end Steve Thornton to the 6, which set up the game's most critical sequence. If the Bears could score a touchdown, it would be just 10–7 Giants and likely a competitive game the rest of the way. On the flip side, if the Giants kept the Bears out of the end zone it would be demoralizing.

On first down, Anderson was stuffed, running just two yards. On second down, Pepper Johnson had his hand in Tomczak's face, causing the quarterback to miss a wide-open Anderson in the end zone and make an errant throw to Muster. On third down, Muster ran a delayed handoff to the Giants 1. The Bears went for it on fourth, and the run never had a chance. The Bears failed to pick up John Washington, who leaped over Bears offensive lineman Jim Covert to tackle Muster for a two-yard loss. Johnson ran into his blocker so hard that his helmet came off.

The Giants, pinned back to their own 1 on the next series, went three-and-out, giving Chicago great field position on the change of possession. The Bears turned that field position into a field goal after Tomczak was able to complete several passes to move the chains.

The Giants made the score 17–3 just before the half on a drive that featured Anderson, Anderson, and more Anderson. In fact, after a 10-yard run from Hostetler to open the drive, the Giants went to Anderson six straight times. He gained 12, nine, nine, three, and four yards, then lost two. Perhaps Parcells was correct when he said the 33-year-old running back wasn't ready to go to the rocking chair just yet.

At the Bears 35, the Giants were staring down their second fourth down of the drive. Hostetler converted on a 10-yard run. Dave Meggett made his own 10-yard run, and after an offsides penalty, the Giants had advanced all the way to the Bears 5. It was all gravy as Hostetler bootlegged to the left and found Howard Cross for the touchdown in the end zone. The touchdown was the only pass on an 11-play, 80-yard drive.

At the half, Chicago didn't panic in the locker room. Tomczak thought the Bears needed to increase the production of Neal Anderson, who carried the ball nine times for 15 yards. One of the reasons that Anderson had done so little was that the Giants knew they needed to stop him in order to win. In addition to the four-man line, they made it difficult for Tomczak to throw to Anderson, as Pepper Johnson stayed with him whenever he tried to catch a pass in the flat. And when he lined up as a receiver, Collins, the Giants' best corner, covered him.

The crushing blow occurred on the Giants' second half opening possession, when the Bears committed a personal foul on the kickoff that gave the Giants the ball at midfield. After no gain on first and second down, Hostetler rolled right, threw back across the grain, and hit Mark Bavaro, who caught the ball about five yards short, but stretched out his body to get the first down. Three plays later, the Giants faced a fourth-and-5 at their own 35 and decided to go for it, a 52-yard field goal into the wind appearing to be nearly impossible. Hostetler, flushed out of the pocket, easily outran Perry for the first down, gaining 12 yards.

"Hostetler really gave us another dimension of mobility that Phil didn't have," said Bavaro. "As much as Phil would try to say that he could run and be a running quarterback, we knew that wasn't his forte."

On the next play, Hostetler completed a 9-yard pass to Baker at the 14. Anderson followed with two runs to the left side for a first down. The Giants were at the Bears 3, with a chance to put the Bears away. Parcells called a bootleg to the right and Hostetler ran two yards before diving the final yard for a touchdown. The cowbells at Giants Stadium rang in harmony with the raspy voice of legendary P.A. announcer Bob Sheppard announcing the touchdown. The Giants had failed to win a playoff game since they beat the Denver Broncos in Super Bowl XX. That drought was over. Now, with about a quarter and a half to play, what the Giants needed more than anything else was to avoid more injuries.

It was something they would have to worry about as soon as the next play. After the kickoff, Bahr himself made the tackle on the returner, but committed the cardinal sin of putting his head down while doing so. Many were doubtful about whether the kicker could play the next week against the 49ers. Collins also hurt his ankle in the third quarter, leaving the game for X-rays. Luckily, he returned to the sidelines in the fourth quarter and was all smiles.

The Giants defense held strong. The Bears simply couldn't get anything going.

The other story of the game was Ottis Anderson. The Giants had acquired him from the Cardinals for insurance purposes behind backup Joe Morris. He was the St. Louis Cardinals' first-round draft pick in 1979 and made it to the Pro Bowl in his first two years. Anderson rushed for more than 1,000 yards in three of his next four seasons, but the Cardinals continued to finish in last place. Giants nose tackle Jim Burt, who was Anderson's college teammate, always teased Anderson when the two teams met. He'd ask Anderson if he was tired of losing and wouldn't it be great if he played for the Giants? When Parcells called Anderson in 1986 to inform him that the Giants had acquired him in a trade, Anderson thought it was a practical joke and hung up the phone. He told the training staff, "You're good. That was one of the best practical jokes I have ever seen." How could he have imagined his old teammate had guessed his fate?

Anderson barely played in the Super Bowl that season, but in the final minutes, with a Giants victory assured, Parcells wanted to put in Anderson to run for a touchdown in the Super Bowl. He told Anderson to replace Morris and congratulated him on a great career, thanking him for coming to New York. Parcells essentially gave Anderson, who ended up running for the touchdown, a send-off speech.

Adding to his embarrassment, in the following season, Mark Ingram was talking with Anderson and asked him whatever happened to the real O.J. Anderson—that really good running back with the Cardinals that he watched while in high school. Anderson told Ingram that he was talking to him.

Ingram replied, "You ain't O.J Anderson. You're *Ottis* Anderson."

It took Ingram a while to be convinced. Anderson remained on the bench for most of the 1987 and 1988 seasons, carrying the ball only 67 times. In 1989, Anderson got another life, becoming the Giants' featured running back and rushing for more than 1,000 yards. But in 1990, he had to split time and eventually lost his starting spot to Hampton, the Giants' first-round draft pick that year. But when Hampton went out of commission with a cracked fibula, Anderson was there to take the field.

Anderson, the oldest running back in the NFL, could wear out a defense, particularly if you gave him the ball multiple times. He was difficult to bring down. He ran for 80 yards on 21 carries including a big run from the Giants 1 to their 11 after they stopped the Bears on fourth down in the third quarter. Anderson, not expecting to play, had subconsciously put on his practice pants and didn't change his attire even after he realized the mistake. After the win, Parcells, ever superstitious, told Anderson that he could start at running back only if he wore his practice pants; Parcells agreed to pay the necessary fine.

The Giants scored their final touchdown with under two minutes left on a Maurice Carthon one-yard touchdown run. Anderson watched from the sidelines as backup RB Lewis Tillman helped the Giants move into scoring position with a mixture of outside and inside runs. Parcells received the Gatorade bath from Walls and Banks. Earlier, on the sidelines, Taylor and Banks said to each other with a smile, "No one thought we could do it, they were sticking a fork in us, but we're back." Parcells said the same thing to Banks with Gatorade all over him. Parcells gave Hostetler praise after the game, telling the New York media that if the Giants lost, it wouldn't be Hostetler's fault. Everyone seemed to believe that the Giants could win with Hostetler.

Perhaps analyst John Madden said it best in the fourth quarter: "I never thought a team could win a Super Bowl with a backup quarterback, but after watching Hostetler I don't know that the Giants *can't* do it."

Summerall responded, "You know he's been here a long time. Seven years." That experience was starting to show. Hostetler wasn't your average backup.

The Giants, though, were already thinking about the NFC championship. "Hey, that was nice," Marshall said. "Now let's get it on with San Francisco."

10.

Showdown in Frisco

ELSEWHERE, THE NEWS WAS BLEAK. On Tuesday, January 15, President George H.W. Bush gave Saddam Hussein a midnight ultimatum to remove his forces from Kuwait or face military action. A lot of discussion centered on whether the championship games should be canceled. *New York Post* columnist Phil Mushnick wrote that the NFL should postpone the playoffs or risk having a guilty conscience forever. He referenced former NFL commissioner Pete Rozelle's infamous decision to play football the Sunday after the Kennedy assassination. Rozelle later admitted that it was his toughest decision as a commissioner.

The debate about whether to cancel sporting events raged, with two competing perspectives. Some argued that the country needed to focus on the crisis and ignore any distractions or entertainments like football. Others felt that life should continue as normal, to show our enemies the resolve of our country. Aside from the academic debate, the NFL and the FBI focused on whether games could be played in a secure atmosphere, without risking the safety of players or fans.

Mushnick, an influential beat writer who wrote the sports television column for the *Post,* felt uneasy about television networks prioritizing their multimillion deals with the NFL over what was in the national interest. He warned of a backlash, noting that networks had nothing to gain except losing millions in television revenue and commercials on deals they were already losing, alluding to how networks often fail to make money from the NFL because of gargantuan rights fees, but needed the NFL's large audience to promote their other shows. Moving forward would simply risk alienating too many people.

117

He also argued that the games wouldn't provide comfort to a nation, especially if Candlestick Park or Tampa Stadium was the target of a terrorist attack. These fears appeared legitimate; in the Middle East, Saddam used scud missiles to attack Israel.

Jerry Izenberg was even more critical than his colleague later in the week when he wrote, "Nothing left but to end this charade, one assumes that the football season is over and if you don't understand why then there is no hope for either of you…. To rally around a football festival as necessary under these circumstances is nothing short of madness. We never had a war with a countdown like this. It is impossible to think of anything less important than playing football this morning."

He continued, "To argue about economics is as banal as it is narrow. In that matter pro football is on its own and to continue to talk about the football tournament would be an insult to America's sensitivity. If we need this as an escape, then God help us."

New director of NFL public relations Greg Aiello says there were never any plans to cancel the game, but the NFL closely listened to what the FBI was telling them. Aiello insists that if the FBI had recommended the league not play, they would have canceled the games.

The NFL issued the following statement: "Candlestick Park and its ground are being secured 24 hours a day through the conclusion of activities on Sunday." Lacking any specific threats, the FBI gave the approval to play—as long as there was extra security at each stadium. As a result, the NFL implemented a lot of security measures that are now routine, like searching fans before they entered the stadium. San Francisco police and the FBI also guarded the stadium for hours prior to kickoff with bomb-sniffing dogs from the FBI checking all outside seats, luxury suites, and the press box.

From the outset of the CBS broadcast on January 20 at Candlestick Park, it was clear this game had special meaning in the national context of war. Thousands of Americans were protesting either for or against the war. On

Saturday, 40,000 peace demonstrators had marched to the San Francisco Civic Center to express their opposition to the conflict. Placards of "Pause for Peace" and "Support Our Troops" were visible throughout the stadium.

The Giants players wore yellow armbands in support of allied forces. Both Giants LB Pepper Johnson and 49ers C Jessie Sapolu had relatives serving overseas and were praying for their safe return. Perhaps Ottis Anderson summed up the mood of his team best when he said the players were loose, concerned about the war, but more focused on the game that everybody expected them to lose (including Mike Ditka, who said that no one was going to beat the 49ers).

The Giants came into the contest eight-point underdogs, but there was some encouraging news during the week. Jumbo Elliott, the Giants All-Pro left tackle, who was hurt in the Giants-49ers regular-season meeting, was playing better after surviving what was deemed a "murderers' row" of tackles and linebackers. That group included Chris Doleman (Minnesota Vikings), Bruce Smith (Buffalo Bills), Ken Harvey (Phoenix Cardinals), Andre Tippett (New England Patriots), and Richard Dent (Chicago Bears).

Giants center Bart Oates often referred to Elliott as a strong country boy and joked that if there was ever a shortage of elephants in India then the Giants could loan Elliott to the Indian government to help reach for the food up in the trees. Asked about the quote years later, Oates hardly remembers.

"Jumbo was a really fun guy to mess around with," said Oates. "He would get really aggravated when you would play a prank on him. He was also someone who got real nervous before games and used to throw up. You would see the stuff all over his helmet and that's how you know that he was ready to play."

It was retribution time for some of the Giants players. Defensive back Everson Walls promised to do a better job of covering wide receiver John Taylor after giving up a touchdown pass in his first game. Walls, along with Dave Duerson and Steve DeOssie, were the three "transplants" in 1990 who added veteran leadership and character to the team. Walls and DeOssie had become close friends after many years together in Dallas, often spending their summers playing pick-up basketball in Texas with mutual friend Ron Springs, who thought of DeOssie as "that crazy white guy" because of his eccentric personality and willingness to do outlandish things. Walls, still an aggressive player, didn't have the speed he once did, but what he lacked in athleticism, he made up for in intelligence.

"With Walls, he is going to gamble sometimes, but he will make smart gambles," Collins said. "At the end of the day, he is going to make a lot more plays than he misses. We expected the 49ers to make one big play against us. The goal was not to give up more than that."

The Giants were excited in the lead-up to the game with San Francisco because of the intensity with which they played the Bears. The whole team was excited. New York's philosophy was clear: bend, but don't break. The Giants knew that the 49ers would stretch the field and make one big offensive play with their talent on offense, but Collins told his teammates it couldn't be more than that. The Giants also had to remain focused because Montana often found the 49ers' third option when his first two options were covered.

Erik Howard and Leonard Marshall were determined to apply a strong pass rush and not let Joe Montana get comfortable in the pocket. Howard, whose hometown is Gilroy, California, "the Garlic Capital of the World," joked about giving his opponents some of that Gilroy garlic to herald his arrival.

Howard rarely spoke on game day. When he arrived at the stadium, he took about 30 minutes putting on his pads and making sure his gear was on correctly. He would stretch out, review his playbook, and, as he puts it, allow all the "fire…within him to explode."

Howard was still upset from the regular season matchup because of what he considered dirty tactics from 49ers offensive lineman Bubba Paris. Asked how he would respond, Howard said, "I am just going to step over his fat butt." Howard felt the 49ers had the dirtiest offensive line in the NFL because they frequently chop blocked, trying to take out players' knees.

"They caused more career-ending injuries than any other group," Howard said. "I also didn't like their fans because I grew up in that area, when the 49ers were really bad in the 1970s, and no one came to the games. All of a sudden when they get good, everyone becomes a 49ers fan."

The 49ers' self-assurance bothered the Giants. Howard, in a loose locker room moment, told the press that he felt an obligation toward history to prevent the 49ers from a three-peat. The comment, along with his picture, ran on the back page of the *New York Post* and *New York Daily News* the next day.

"It was a total shock to me. That statement becoming big news without me having thought about it beforehand was kind of cool," said Howard.

When the Giants arrived at Candlestick Park, they experienced the 49ers' arrogance firsthand, encountering suitcases with "Tampa" labeled on them, as 49ers players arranged Super Bowl tickets for their family. Numerous players, particularly Banks, discussed how the 49ers viewed this game against the Giants as a coronation and New York just another team they had to beat. Former 49ers coach Bill Walsh, two years removed from coaching, predicted the Giants would be unable to stop the 49ers' passing game.

Said Ronnie Lott, "We were really excited about the opportunity to three-peat. We knew it had never been done before."

The Giants, of course, disagreed. "We are not coming out here to send the 49ers off to the Super Bowl. We have a purpose," Pepper Johnson said.

Two days before the game, Montana missed Friday's practice with flu-like symptoms. On Saturday, he came to the walk-through and went home. Apparently, one of Montana's children had the flu and Montana had caught it. Still, when the Giants left New York on Friday around 2:00 PM, they left the only place in the world where anyone had given them a chance to win.

San Francisco head coach George Seifert admitted publicly that he thought his team was too conservative in the first game, even if they had won. So offensive coordinator Mike Holmgren opened up the offense, giving Montana more places to throw even when his receivers were covered. The 49ers hoped that the return of receiver Mike Sherrard would give them yet another option if the Giants doubled-teamed Jerry Rice and Taylor.

Mark Collins, though, was experienced at covering Rice. In Week 13, he held him to just one catch. Collins understood that the most dangerous aspect of Rice was his quickness; once the receiver created separation and broke on a route, he was difficult to stop. Collins' strategy was to bump Rice at the line of scrimmage, making it difficult for him to make a move and have open space in order to cut. Knowing that Collins was on Rice and Walls was responsible for Taylor, Montana knew he had to find other options.

And so the contest began.

On San Francisco's opening drive, Montana did indeed find a supporting cast. His first three completions were good to fullback Tom Rathman, Sherrard, and tight end Brent Jones. Collins' strategy was working. Later in the first drive, he let Rice catch the ball—but hit him shortly thereafter for a one-yard loss. The drive was stalled after LT and Gary Reasons were able to get pressure up the middle and force Montana to throw the ball incomplete. The 49ers connected on a 47-yard field goal to take a 3–0 lead. The 49ers threw seven times and ran twice, a mixture that reflected their normal play calling and lack of confidence in running back Roger Craig.

If there was any doubt whether Jeff Hostetler's performance the week before was a fluke, it was answered on the Giants' opening possession. Facing third-and-13, Hostetler rolled to the right after being chased and found wide receiver Mark Ingram for a 20-yard gain. It was a play, without a doubt, made by the quarterback and not the wide receiver. On the next play, Hostetler completed another rollout to tight end Mark Bavaro for seven yards.

Many pundits later commented that this championship game was perhaps the most physical ever played. That physicality was established early on in two plays on opposite ends of the ball: Johnson upending Rathman on the 49ers' opening possession, and safety Ronnie Lott laying out Giants wideout Ingram on the Giants' first series.

The Giants successfully drove inside the 49ers 10-yard line on the power running of Ottis Anderson. They tried a trick play, hoping to score an early touchdown, but fell flat. Hostetler pitched the ball to Dave Meggett, who threw a perfect pass that fullback Maurice Carthon dropped in the end zone. New York was forced to settle for a field goal and a 3–3 tie.

Montana was struggling to find open receivers because the Giants rushed only four, or at most five, guys and dropped the rest in coverage. This defensive scheme allowed for few passing lanes with the linebackers occupying the middle and the defensive backs occupying the deep passing lanes. Montana's only option was to dump the ball off in the flat to a running back or a fullback. It was by design. Bill Belichick didn't think that players like Rathman and Jones could beat them, so they were the ones often left in single coverage with a linebacker.

Early in the second quarter, Collins knocked away another pass intended for Rice, staying with the receiver and catching up to knock the ball away after Rice had created a little separation.

Late in the second quarter, the Giants had put together a 14-play drive with a mixture of Anderson runs and short passes to Bavaro that led to another field goal.

Montana responded with his signature two-minute magic—finally completing a long pass to Rice, good for 19 yards, and then ran seven yards to the 40. After a five-yard pass to Craig, the Giants made a costly mistake. Howard wrapped his arms around Montana and threw him to the ground; he was flagged for a personal foul, which moved San Francisco all the way to the Giants 20. Angered by the call, Marshall beat Paris to the inside and sacked Montana for a 10-yard loss on the next play. At the end of the play, Paris jumped on the pile, causing Marshall to throw a punch at Paris. The officials missed the late hit and its aftermath. But Marshall was angry that Paris landed on him after he felt the play was over.

At the half, CBS News anchor Dan Rather gave an update on the progress of the U.S. war effort. Two scud missiles hit the U.S. base in Dhahran, Saudi Arabia, and Riyadh, the Saudi capital. Allied operations were delayed because of poor weather, stopping numerous bombing missions whose primary target was to take out the scud missile launchers.

"What still amazes me about the 49ers game is before the game, in the locker room, we were watching the Bills blow out [the Los Angeles Raiders] and I thought to myself, *There is no way we are going to beat the Bills if we go to the Super Bowl.* I knew our defense wouldn't allow them to score 50 points, but I didn't think our offense, which most games seemed to score about 14 points, could compete with the Bills offense," said Bavaro.

"I also remember the Gulf War was going on and I thought, *What could be more pointless than playing football at this moment?* People were talking about all these crazy scenarios like nuclear warfare and it made football seem like it wasn't that big of a deal.

"I also don't think there would have been a lot of negative reaction if we lost. I didn't expect to beat the 49ers, as they were on a roll, looking to head to threepeat."

Despite it all, there was still another half of football to be played. The 49ers showed their strong pass rush on the Giants' opening drive, giving Hostetler constant pressure. Charles Haley beat right tackle Doug Riesenberg on an inside rush to sack Hostetler on third down, forcing a Giants punt that gave the 49ers great field position at the San Francisco 41. On the next play, Walls gambled and tried to make the interception on a pass to Taylor. He missed the interception and Taylor came up with it, running 61 yards for a touchdown to make it 13–6.

Hostetler responded with a 19-yard completion to Ingram, but the 49ers run defense stiffened, holding Anderson to a one-yard gain. The drive appeared over, but then Dave Waymer was called for a pass interference penalty after holding Bavaro. The Giants completed another third-and-10 to Bavaro over the middle to the 49ers 37. Anderson ran seven yards to put the Giants in field-goal range and Bahr connected from 46 yards to make it 13–9.

On the next drive, the 49ers tried to change the pace with a no-huddle offense, but a Taylor sack prevented anything from happening.

Early in the fourth quarter, luck seemed to turn away from the Giants when Dave Meggett returned a 49ers punt to the Giants 45. Anderson had two runs of nine and 27 yards to put the Giants in the red zone, but then Bahr missed a 36-yard field goal. Madden declared from the broadcast booth that the Giants couldn't win unless they scored a touchdown.

The Giants defense prevented the 49ers from scoring on their next possession and got the ball back. Soon after, they suffered what appeared to be a crushing blow when Hostetler completed a pass over the middle to Ingram but was hit at the knees by Jim Burt as he threw the ball. Many Giants players quietly admitted that the play probably wasn't dirty because of Burt's momentum, but the the offense used it as a source of motivation. LT screamed from the sidelines, "If you are going to hurt one of our quarterbacks, we will hurt one of your quarterbacks!"

Backup quarterback Matt Cavanaugh (one of the team's biggest jokesters) temporarily replaced Hostetler. On his first pass, Cavanaugh overthrew Bavaro by about 10 yards. The Giants needed Hostetler back—and quickly. When the training staff evaluated Hostetler, Parcells walked to the bench, a rare act for a head coach, to offer words of encouragement. Hostetler had a slight hyperextension in his right knee, but with the help of three trainers, he started to move on the sidelines and took some snaps from center Bart Oates.

San Francisco got the ball back, and as Hostetler recovered the Giants defense was thinking about creating a turnover. Johnson delivered a hard hit on Taylor over the middle on second down to force and a third-and-10. At the beginning of the third down play, Montana had a lot of time. He wanted to throw to Rice, but Collins jumped the route; Montana realized that if he threw the pass it would probably be intercepted. The coverage allowed the Giants defense to pressure Montana, who eluded Taylor before Marshall hit Thomas with maximum force. Marshall was on the other side of the field when he started running full speed to hit Montana. Marshall's 290 pounds collided with Montana, and the quarterback fumbled. The loose ball went through Collins' open arms, but the 49ers came up with it. When asked about the play the next day, Montana said he didn't remember anything and would have to look at the tape.

"I wasn't trying to hurt him. I looked at myself as a paid mercenary, trying to hit anything that moved on the football field," Marshall said.

The recovery gave the 49ers a chance to punt, and the Giants took over at their own 35 with 9:17 left. After Anderson gained three yards on first down, Hostetler, back in the game, narrowly escaped a sack from two 49ers defenders around him, completing a five-yard run. The Giants needed one yard for a first down, but nose tackle Michael Carter burst through the line of scrimmage to tackle Anderson for a one-yard loss. The Giants had to punt.

Or did they? Coaches gave Gary Reasons instructions to fake the punt if he thought there was an angle with an open hole. Reasons quickly recognized that the 49ers defensive line was geared toward the left. The right side would be open. He took the snap and jolted forward, gaining 30 yards in the process. Unfortunately, the Giants went three-and-out after the fake, but made it 13–12 on Matt Bahr's fourth field goal of the day.

Steve Young entered the game and seemed supremely confident, completing a 25-yard pass to Jones. Roger Craig then looked like the Roger Craig of old, running for two consecutive first downs. With 2:40 remaining, the 49ers seemed in control. Marshall didn't see it that way. He started screaming "one minute until Tampa." He repeated it for good measure in the Giants huddle.

He sensed the 49ers would call Spread 35, an off-tackle run to the right behind Paris. Marshall told LT to get the tight end, and that he would take care of Paris. Howard screamed to his teammates that someone needed to make a play. Ninety-eight percent of the time, Howard knew the play based on the offensive linemen's stances; the position of 49ers guard Guy McIntyre told him it would be a run right. Howard remembered what his coaches told him in practice all year about how to handle a double team on a running play: jab at the center, drop to one knee, and fly up the middle to make the play.

The goal was to prevent Craig from bouncing outside and force him toward the middle of the Giants defense where Howard could create a fumble. Sure enough, that's what happened. Craig ran straight into Howard, who fell to one knee to fool Sapolu before standing up to reach between his two blockers, grab Craig at his midsection, and force his helmet on the ball, which skyrocketed up in the air and landed in the arms of LT.

"We just needed some luck and I was the right guy there at the right time," LT said.

The Giants had new life and one last chance at the Super Bowl. Hostetler told his teammates on the sidelines, "We can do this." Just before the offense went onto the field, Anderson looked at Ingram with a sharp grin. Just moments before, Ingram was whining on the sideline about how he always dreamed of playing in the Super Bowl and would likely miss his closest opportunity. Anderson responded, "Ingy, it's my destiny to go the Super Bowl." Fifteen years earlier as an undergraduate at the University of Miami, Anderson vowed that if he ever played in a Super Bowl in Florida, he would be the MVP. Anderson, who despite a bad groin rushed for more than 1,000 yards in 1989, thought the chances of achieving his dream were over when the Rams eliminated the Giants in the playoffs that season. But then Carthon told him the Super Bowl was in Tampa the following year. Anderson had declared to Carthon that his destiny would come true.

"I don't remember any of this," Carthon said jokingly. "But I trust O.J. that it all happened."

What happened next was nothing short of magical. Hostetler, chased out of the pocket, completed a 19-yard pass to Bavaro to the 49ers 40. Bavaro felt that he was one second away from breaking a tackle that would have allowed him to run for a touchdown. "Sometimes you feel like if you get that one extra inch of separation you could go all the way and that is exactly how I felt," he said.

"I have so much respect for Mark," Lott said. "He really was one of the premier tight ends of his era. You knew that if you didn't play your best game he was going to take advantage."

49ers defensive end Kevin Fagan tackled Anderson for a four-yard loss. Then Hostetler rolled to the right to find Stephen Baker for a 13-yard completion to the 29. Baker should have been penalized for offensive pass interference, as he pushed Pollard away, but he got the no-call. Anderson bulled his way downfield for a first down to the 27. Anderson added two more. A Hostetler QB sneak moved the ball to the 24 and the Giants called their final timeout. There were four seconds left on the clock.

With a 42-yard field goal separating the Giants from the Super Bowl, all the players could do was hope. They had done all they could do. Collins, Johnson, Walls, Roger Brown, and Dave Duerson formed a prayer circle and looked the other way. Collins was somewhat frustrated that all the Giants' hard work came down to one kick. He thought about all that could go wrong. Parcells and Belichick paced back and forth on the sidelines. When they crossed paths, they said nothing to each other. Ingram knelt alone with his hands up in the air and everyone left Bahr alone, not wanting to say anything to him, even when the 49ers called the standard timeout to ice the kicker.

Broadcaster Pat Summerall, a former Giants kicker, summarized the emotional difference between making and missing the kick as Bahr walked around alone. "It's a lonely world, believe me," he said. "If he should miss, it will be an eternity. And if he should make it, he will never know that he got on the airplane."

Hostetler, who was the holder, knew that if he could catch the ball and get the laces down correctly, Bahr could make the kick. Any holder has another motivation in this situation. No holder wants to be remembered for botching his team's chances of going to the Super Bowl.

The snap and hold were perfect. And while the kick was a little left, there was little doubt about if it was good or not—as evidenced by the sudden silence of the 49ers crowd shortly after the ball left Bahr's foot. Many 49ers fans insist that Candlestick was so eerily quiet after Bahr's kick that you could hear the Giants players screaming and yelling in the stands.

Pat Summerall stated the obvious with his trademark gusto, "The kick is good and there will be no threepeat." Giants players streamed onto the field toward Bahr, who already had Reasons and Taylor all over him.

The Giants were headed to the Super Bowl.

When Hostetler arrived at his locker he said a little prayer, thanking the Lord for the opportunity. The fun started soon thereafter. Phil Simms put Icy Hot in Hostetler's underwear, which he realized during the postgame locker room celebration. He immediately suspected Simms, since he had become used to his pranks over the years, but he could only laugh. Simms also once put a potato in the engine of Hostetler's car so he couldn't start it. Another time, Simms had deposited the blue powder that the FBI uses to mark stolen items inside Hostetler's helmet, so it would rub all over his face during practice. When Hostetler took the helmet off, his face was covered in blue powder that he couldn't get off.

"It took almost a week to wash off," said Collins, who, along with the rest of his teammates, was laughing as hard as he could. Collins was no stranger to the Icy Hot prank, either. He had once put the gel in Taylor's jock strap, eliciting expletives that were too much, even for Taylor.

Madden wanted to interview Hostetler and he agreed—only if the Giants would hold the bus. His teammates told him not to worry. Or so he thought. And Parcells and the rest of the team left without the quarterback who led them to the Super Bowl. Madden gave Hostetler a ride in his cruiser, arranging a police escort from the highway to the tarmac where the plane was sitting.

"Madden saved the day, because I didn't even know what airport we were at," Hostetler said.

As Hostetler walked onto the plane, Parcells sat in the first row with a look of bewildered amusement and shock on his face—not unlike his feelings toward the quarterback's play in the latter part of that storied Giants season.

11.

The Marshall Plan

IN SOME WAYS, THINGS HAVEN'T CHANGED for Leonard Marshall. Facing multiple obstacles in business and with his foundation, the Game Plan, Marshall compares it to overcoming two or three offensive linemen in the Giants 3-4 defense, when he was double-teamed on every play. He uses the same motto to describe both situations: *Nothing is easy, so I just keep prying and trying.* He made three Pro Bowls and finished his career with 83.5 sacks. From 1985 to 1991, he had only one season with fewer than eight sacks. He won NFL Defensive Lineman of the Year with 15.5 sacks in 1985.

He is often remembered for the hit he made on Joe Montana in the 1990 NFC Championship Game, which ended Montana's career in San Francisco and helped the Giants win their second Super Bowl. But the tough-as-nails lineman, who was unafraid of speaking his mind in New York when he criticized teammates Jim Burt and LT after the Giants won their first Super Bowl, is showing his softer side now. He wants to help the teammates and opponents who, in retirement, now struggle with finances and health insurance payments.

He has a speech prepared for anyone who is willing to listen about how retired players have been mistreated. He discusses how the average NFL pension is below the federal poverty line for a two-person household and the difficulty players have with receiving disability. The average NFL career lasts only a little more than three years, which until recently was the minimum amount of time required to earn a pension. Most NFL players will be divorced within two years of leaving the NFL, and within three years they are likely to be broke.

"There are these statistics, but what is more powerful is what I have seen with my own eyes," Marshall says. "Guys just don't know what to do when they retire. Today the situation is a lot better, but when players retired in the '70s, '80s they had tremendous health care costs and were often out of money."

Marshall has found a way to make money after retirement from the league. He returned to business this past year to sell home health products like neck and knee braces to Wal-Mart. Marshall organized a supply chain from China to Canada to the U.S. to help make the products quickly and efficiently. His company does $460,000 worth of business each month. Not bad for a new company. Ironically, he refuses to do business with other players unless they are willing to work hard and share his business mentality.

"In general, I stay away from players. They are finicky," he says. He understands why many of them don't succeed after football. "You have to be willing to work. A lot of players think they can just show up and make the money. For the most part, that approach doesn't work once you leave the NFL."

Marshall likes to be involved in multiple projects at one time, never wanting to do just one thing. Some probably want him to throw his BlackBerry away. He is, after all, always on it—discussing his latest business venture or a new charitable enterprise. He's addicted to it—so addicted that when his cell phone and BlackBerry ran out of charge at a restaurant in New York City, he begged the waitress for a table near a plug so he could talk on his cell phone in between bites.

The conversation often follows a similar pattern.

"Can I have more potatoes?"

"We should sell her a $75,000 insurance policy, because we have a chance of making $200,000."

It's what first struck me about Marshall—his grit and determination. He complained about how the league treated retired players, so I expected to hear that he had lost most of his own money through poor investments and received little help from the NFL. Marshall, however, is a successful businessman who is simply concerned about helping retired players in dire need. After a successful post-football career, Marshall devotes most of his time to fighting for the rights of his former teammates and opponents whom he played against in the 1980s. He knows the players' rights well and has met with Commissioner Roger Goodell several times.

What bothered him most was how the NFL's marketing machine turned players into gladiators, an image that many players "buy into" until well after they retire. Realizing too late that it doesn't exist anymore, they hold onto their press clippings and the dwindling praise as proof of what once was. Quickly, though, players like Marshall realize that stardom is short-lived and that their lifestyle as an NFL player is no longer sustainable. Often, by that point, the money is gone.

"You'd be surprised how quickly money disappears, particularly if you spent a lot as a player, when you have no income coming in," Marshall said. "You get so used to the big salaries."

It's easy to flip on the TV and see former players like Phil Simms, Shannon Sharpe, or Dan Marino, and expect great jobs in retirement that will earn them millions every year. Marshall points out that these on-air examples are the exception, not the rule. Marshall has compiled 200 pages of articles about the difficulties facing retired players, documenting every conceivable problem: unemployment, divorce, concussions, financial hardship, obesity, and so on.

He set up a foundation, the Game Plan, to help retired players in dire need pay for their health care costs. Players who retired after 1998 receive five years of health insurance, but those who retired before then often received only subsidized health care that they had to pay for. Marshall specifically targets five conditions that retired players suffer from disproportionately: dementia, Alzheimer's disease, concussions, chronic back pain, and vertigo. His goal is to raise between $1.2 and $3 million in order to help 100 retired players a year. His bigger dream, though, is to help NYU build a $30 million neurological trauma center to study the effects of head injuries on the brain.

"Paying for health insurance is one of the biggest worries that retired players face," Marshall said. "The cost for an NFL player to insure himself and his family can be very high."

He also set up a for-profit organization to help coach retired players on how to succeed in business. MBA professors will create a customized program for each player at a cost of $12,500. He wants the league to pay one-third, the players to pay one-third, and the NFL Players' Association to pay for a third. Fans can donate to their favorite players at www.yourcause.com. The title is only fitting, as players, he says, receive little guidance or direction when they leave the NFL. Many players have solely focused on football since they were young children. Marshall's challenges, though, have been enormous.

The NFL has rejected a lot of Marshall's ideas, including the MBA program, and funding has been limited. Additionally, Marshall is one of myriad players to help set up a foundation for retired players. The truth is that most of the others have delivered little in the way of assistance to those who need it most. The most publicized charity, Gridiron Greats, founded by Mike Ditka, has donated almost no money to retired players in dire need. Most of its raised funds have been spent on administration.

Said former Green Bay Packers great Jerry Kramer, who was involved with Gridiron Greats, "One of the biggest issues is finding the players who actually need the money. A lot of them don't want to come out of the woodwork. You might see them at an alumni tournament, but then never hear from them. Often, it is not until a player has serious dementia that you will see his wife call or caretaker call to say, 'We need help.' The other big issue is staying united, so we don't sound like 50 guys throwing mud pies in the woods."

Marshall's motivation is a reflection of his former coach Bill Parcells. In the back of his mind, he can still hear Parcells yelling, or see in his mind's eye the sharp glare that was the coach's trademark. It's difficult to play eight years for Parcells and not be influenced one way or another. Marshall remembers Parcells' tired cliché of "I go by what I see" when he tries to help former teammates and opponents. He refuses to be known as another successful player who sat idly by during a crisis.

"He taught me what drive is," Marshall said.

After Marshall retired he was nearly broke; like so many players, he made investments based on the recommendations of other players that didn't turn out well. But Marshall founded Pro Star Athletic, a company that manufactured team apparel, which he later sold for more than $2 million. The company succeeded because of Marshall's work ethic. He attended numerous apparel conventions, marketing his T-shirts with autographed player signatures. He created publicity for the products and convinced stores like Kmart, J.C. Penney, Wal-Mart, and Sears to sell them.

Baltimore Ravens wide receiver Donte Stallworth once joked about an investment culture that led players to invest in anything and everything. Stallworth was even asked to invest in funeral homes. It's something former Buffalo Bills nose tackle Fred Smerlas knows a lot about. According to Smerlas, many players invest in houses, cars, or restaurants—things they know nothing about. Players often think that because they are successful in football, they can duplicate that same success in business. Most of the time, they fail. Smerlas warns current players that the money isn't infinite; it will eventually stop. He encourages players to protect their assets with low-risk investments. Players must also realize that they are on the bottom of the totem pole, not the top, when they start in business.

"Players often think they know everything," Smerlas said. "I tell them to approach business with attitude of 'I know nothing.'"

It's a lesson Parcells emphasized to Marshall.

"He really motivated me to get back on track," Marshall said. "He told me, 'Marshall, I never saw you get outworked as a player. I don't want to see you get outworked now.'"

Marshall admires the "hell out of Parcells." Part of him is jealous of his career path and his ability to keep making money. While Marshall enjoys helping retired players, he admires former players like Baltimore Ravens general manager Ozzie Newsome, who translated his success on the playing field to the front office.

Marshall wants to be on the fast track for an administrative job—but how to get on it is the problem. Coaching opportunities, unlike in the NBA and MLB, are few and far between for former NFL players. The NFL, as opposed to other sports, expects players to work their way up. They don't just hand out jobs.

"I would love to be a defensive line coach somewhere, become a defensive coordinator, a head coach, and then head into an administrative job like Parcells," Marshall said. "Too bad the process might take 20 years or more."

Added former Bills linebacker Darryl Talley playfully, "I don't think Marshall knows what Marshall wants."

More than anything, Marshall respects how Parcells continues to market himself as the premier executive to turn a team around. Just ask Miami Dolphins owner Wayne Huizenga and Dallas Cowboys owner Jerry Jones. The Miami Dolphins paid Parcells $1.5 million to be their president. Jerry Jones paid Parcells more than $5 million to coach and return the Cowboys to respectability. Records and Super Bowls are what measure success in the NFL. Few remember the nice coaches, but most remember the successful ones like Vince Lombardi, Chuck Noll, Tom Landry, and Bill Walsh. That success is ultimately what players respect, regardless of a coach's personality.

"Parcells was kind of like the sheriff behind the whole operation," Marshall said. "He knew how to motivate players, and he had a coaching staff filled with great teachers. They made things simpler, so when you got on the field you felt like you had an edge."

Marshall often referred to Parcells as "Dollar Bill," because in Marshall's mind, money helped motivate the coach. It was that Dollar Bill image that created a love-hate relationship between Marshall and Parcells. When he was called "Dollar Bill," Parcells jokingly responded, "Marshall, you are the only one to have my number." In an odd way, though, Marshall admired his tactics. After all, he turned an overweight, immature player from Louisiana into an All-Pro. During his first training camp, Marshall gave Kevin Croke, the teenage son of Giants director of media relations Ed Croke, the keys to his new Saab so he could bring him McDonald's cheeseburgers after curfew. Parcells immediately assigned Marshall to a dietician who put him on a high-protein, medium-carbohydrate diet. Maybe he didn't like how cunning his coach could be, but he appreciated his motivational skills. Marshall held out before the 1990 season because of a contract dispute. Parcells told him, "Tim Mara is not giving you any more money."

"Then your fat ass is going to have to gain 50 pounds and play the defensive line," Marshall thought about telling Parcells. To make matters worse, LT was holding out at the same time. Marshall spent August playing golf in Louisiana instead of attending training camp. He spoke with the Saints about joining their defensive line. Marshall thought he was headed to New Orleans for a more exciting 4-3 scheme and one of the best defensive lines in football. But Parcells needed his two best defensive players, and both received their salary increases.

"When these two players were holding out, it really meant that we were without two cornerstones of our defense," Parcells said. "Beyond that, we really missed the leadership that they provided."

Parcells told Marshall that he would "stick it to him." Marshall wondered *I got what I wanted, what is Parcells going to do now?* But Parcells remembered that Marshall prided himself on his consistency. From 1985 to 1989, Marshall started in every game in which he played (missing three games to injury). As retribution for the holdout, Parcells refused to start Marshall in his first 10 games, always putting him in on the second play.

"Can you imagine doing that? That a— ruined my consecutive game streak," said Marshall. "But in a way you had to admire him, because he would do anything just to show who is the boss."

Marshall recorded 4.5 sacks and was named as an alternate in the Pro Bowl, in which he eventually got to play. He made potentially the most devastating hit in NFL history when he clobbered Joe Montana on a delayed backside hit. He also had a sack in the Super Bowl, especially impressive since the Giants only rushed three players the entire game and he was double-teamed on almost every play.

Today, he approaches the business world with the same hustle and ferocity with which he attacked NFL quarterbacks. He told me, "I have to hustle." He sets a goal of making $5,000 per week. Most weeks, he meets it. He started with his apparel business. He has since tried the mortgage business, the life insurance business, and even the stock market.

"You feel this obligation to provide the best lifestyle you can for your family. You want your daughter to go to that Hannah Montana concert, your wife to have nice jewelry, and to be able to travel whenever you want," he said. "The difficult part is keeping that up when you retire. Players often spend like they are still playing, yet the money isn't coming."

"It can dry up real fast if you don't watch it," said former Buffalo Bills running back Thurman Thomas.

Older and wiser, he understands that stardom is short-lived. Former Los Angeles Dodgers pitcher Sandy Koufax famously said, "Baseball is what you do until you grow up." That phrase resonated with Marshall, and he believes the same is true with football. He refused to cannibalize himself when he retired, trying to fit into his old uniform at trade shows or dedicating his life to signing his name on a football card. He moved on, afraid of being that guy from his childhood past.

He attributes his hustle to his childhood in Franklin, Louisiana. He had five brothers and sisters. His father worked as a shipyard foreman and was a part-time bartender at a local saloon. Growing up in the early and mid-1970s, Marshall was largely shielded by his family from racial discrimination. He resented laziness, not the white establishment.

"[My father] did an amazing job," Marshall says. "I used to play basketball with a diverse group of kids in other towns. You name it: white, black, or Hispanic. In many ways, I didn't sense what was going on in the world around me. I changed high schools three different times, but I never really asked why. They just told me that was the way it was."

Early on, his father instilled in him the importance of education. Marshall knew it could be his only ticket out of Franklin. "I told him education was the key," Leonard Marshall Sr. said. "That was something they can't take away from you. I also told him I would kick his ass if I found him using his race as an excuse for not achieving what he wanted to achieve."

Marshall quickly noticed the difference between success and failure. He saw strangers passed out on the street, spending their last dollars on alcohol. He pledged that would never be him. Despite his busy work schedule, Marshall Sr. spent time with his family and made sure they never had to worry about food.

"I will never forget the day he came home at the age of seven and said, 'I don't want to be like that guy on the street corner,'" Marshall's mother said. "I was so shocked that such a young boy would be so smart."

Marshall Sr. in many ways stands in contrast to his son, a product of a different generation. Marshall Sr., who experienced the worst type of racism in the 1930s and 1940s, witnessed laws that prevented blacks from using the same swimming pool as whites and factories that paid blacks a tenth of the wages they paid whites. He was more of a pragmatist than a dreamer, worried about feeding his family and paying the rent.

He was skeptical when, one Sunday after church while watching football, little Marshall told him, "Daddy, one day you will be watching me play football on television."

"Come on, you ain't serious," he said.

Marshall was determined to make it. Coaches and teammates noticed his prolific speed as a youngster. He was faster than anyone and could leap higher.

His mother thought basketball was his best sport, but he started eating a lot more food in high school. The summer after his senior year of high school, he was staying with his cousin Lillian. He showed that he could out-eat and out-run everyone in the neighborhood. Then her son challenged Marshall to a race, saying he could beat him because he was so big.

"He never made that mistake again," said Lillian.

After retirement, Marshall feared becoming the passed-out alcoholic he saw on the streets growing up. He knew that when an active player acts like a bum he is cool, but when a retired player acts like a bum he is a bum because he is yesterday's news. Today, he sees too many teammates who are simply out of money.

"A lot of times, guys are not prepared for their end," Marshall said. "They think that it is going to last forever."

That "it" is the luxury of being a professional athlete.

"In many ways, playing in the NFL is like being a child," Marshall said. "Everything is done for you. They tell you when to eat, how to eat, when to get up, what time to be places."

When Marhsall sees former players struggle, he doesn't think, *What is wrong with my former teammates?*, but rather, *How did the system fail these players to such an extent?* His intent in documenting this story is not to embarrass any teammate, but rather to simply ask why a player could be so successful on the field but have such difficulty off it.

It's a question that other teammates have asked as well. Mark Bavaro, former All-Pro Giants tight end, said, "It is rough getting out of football. You think the NFL prepares you for life after football, but it doesn't."

Bavaro, who wrote a fictional book about a player coping with the end of his career, says that in 1990 he was exactly like the character in his book. He could have missed the season because his knee was collapsing. Doctors told him that he needed bone graft surgery to replace the hole in his knee.

"They were nervous," Bavaro said. "It could have collapsed at any moment, even during a simple drill in practice. In August, the hole wasn't that bad, but by October the doctors said it was amazing that I was still able to play. I knew that the knee could collapse even if I made one wrong step."

Bavaro thought about having surgery in the middle of the season, but chose to put it off until the end of the season. The Giants told Bavaro that they wouldn't renew his contract in 1991 under any conditions. Bavaro had surgery one week after the Giants won Super Bowl XXV. He told George Young that he would miss the 1991 season and that if he could return in 1992, he would sign with the Giants. Bavaro wanted about $300,000 to rehab with the Giants, not a lot of money for a player of his caliber. Young gave him a puzzled look as if to say, *Why would we ever do that?*

"I told my wife it would be a great a way to go out if I could win a Super Bowl and finish with two rings for my career. I tried, though, not to let any of my teammates know, and I didn't even think a lot of the coaches knew—just really my family and the doctors."

"The other difficult thing was the coaches were much tougher back then than they are today about practicing. Even as bad as my knee was, they still wanted me working with the team every day. They just wouldn't allow us to show up on game days."

Bavaro, like Marshall, talks about how the NFL is an insular world.

"For the 10 years that you play," Marshall says, "that locker room is your cocoon. You always have a teammate that is there to help bail you out."

"Even if you are lazy, someone is always kicking your ass to play harder."

"It's that motivation that players often miss. Real-world and NFL diplomacy are so different," said former Giants coach Jim Fassel.

Many players have trouble meeting their benefit deadlines simply because they don't have a coach standing over them urging them to do it.

"A lot of players are denied benefits because they can't get their paperwork in on time," Smerlas said. "The league will say you need to have this form in on this particular date to be eligible for a program, and more guys miss the deadline than you would think."

"The classic image of retired players is someone that has a trophy wife, plays golf, and has little worry about money," Marshall said. "That reality couldn't be further from the truth." Too many ex-players he knew were broke, others lacked health insurance, and most were divorced.

That direct deposit of $200,000 every week ends, and you maintain a lifestyle that is no longer sustainable. Even more difficult, the adulation of fans makes you continue to believe in your star power. People still beg him for autographs, others tried to steal his Super Bowl rings at the airport.

"You really have to watch your back every second," Marshall said.

It's also challenging to walk away from what has been a lifelong talent at such an early age. Players have their whole lives ahead of them, but no guidance as to what to do. "Imagine telling a doctor or lawyer that their career had to end at 33, 34, or 35," said Marshall. "A typical career spans 30 or 40 years, but in the NFL it is five years, if you are lucky."

Marshall teaches players to separate themselves from the past. Players, he says, need to know how to leverage their image as a professional athlete, not how to bask in it. It isn't simple, he says, but if a player is willing to work, it isn't difficult either. The bottom line is few companies want another entitled, lazy athlete. Marshall believes most players undersell themselves, which is why he wants to establish a program that partners players with companies. He tells guys that if they can succeed in the NFL, they can succeed in the workplace. In a way, he says, the NFL is more difficult.

"There are so many skills that a player learns in the NFL that can be used in the workplace, like punctuality, attention to detail, and a thick skin. But many forget that when they go for a job interview."

Marshall struggles to comprehend why kick-returning specialist Dave Meggett has had numerous runs-in with the law, or why wide receiver Mark Ingram is behind bars. Many ask him about sympathy. Should the public feel bad for players who made more in one year, in some cases, than many Americans make over a lifetime?

A tough question, but Marshall answers it vehemently, ranting about how retired players have been "screwed over" by the NFLPA, noting they have the worst pension benefits in all of sports, a system that fails to provide its ex-players with health insurance.

"People really idolize athletes in our culture so when they drink or cheat on their wife, a lot of people consider them cool," Smerlas said. "But when you leave football you are considered just another drunken bum."

Former athletes, he says, are pigeonholed sometimes, a stereotype than can be difficult to shake. Marshall has watched many of his teammates experience bitter divorces because ex-players can no longer support their wives' lifestyles.

"Oftentimes they marry because of who they are, not so much the type of person you are," Marshall says. "They know it will bring them a lot of wealth. But once that wealth stops when a player retires, it is difficult for the marriage to sustain itself. Plus, there is no longer the thrill of being married to an NFL player. Unless you were a superstar, you are just another ex-player looking for a job."

Said former Giant Harry Carson, who played with Marshall on the 1986 Giants Super Bowl team, "They aren't really married to *you*. They are often married to all the accoutrements that come with being married to an NFL player: the money, the lifestyle, and the status that comes with it. When you take that away, what are you—the player—left with?"

Statistics show that a high percentage of retired players are divorced. Smerlas thinks players, like recovering alcoholics, almost need a rehabilitation facility to adjust from the pampered lifestyle of an NFL player. This includes even simple things, like diet. Players are often fed breakfast, lunch, and dinner at their team facilities. Never preparing their own meals, they gain little understanding of nutrition.

"When you play, especially if you are good player, the organization really wants to do everything for you, just so you can play on Sunday," Marshall says. "The interests of the player and the organization are really aligned. But once you get out, there is no teammate to hold your hand anymore."

12.

Game Plan Magic

IT IS STILL CONSIDERED MAYBE THE BEST GAME PLAN in NFL history, and one must travel to the Pro Football Hall of Fame in Canton, Ohio, in order to see it. No photocopies are allowed—even if you spend thousands on a plane ticket and have a research appointment. Only then are you able to read what almost seems like a foreign language.

The word that is repeatedly used in reference to the plan is "brilliant." And the thing that makes it all the more impressive is how quickly the Giants put it together. Despite Parcells' belief that you should never look ahead, he did just that as his team prepared for San Francisco, drawing up game plans for both the Bills and Raiders. By the time the Giants flew from San Francisco to Tampa, advance scout Tim Rooney had completed a massive scouting report and put the observations onto his laptop. The massive scouting report contained all the formations the Bills had used against the Raiders and how many times they used them.

"It allowed us to jump right into the game plan, so we didn't feel bad for ourselves about not having the week off," Parcells said.

After the Super Bowl, the Bills would admit that their preparation was a day or two behind the Giants, who were able to start practice a day earlier, causing Bills coach Marv Levy to miss Tuesday's media day and receive a $5,000 fine from then–NFL commissioner Paul Tagliabue. Levy lost track of time as he finished the Bills game plan for their opening practice on Wednesday. Levy could have made it, but realized he would be late so he stayed away from practice altogether. Levy, though, used his deft sense of humor the next day to deflect any lingering controversy when he opened his press conference by saying he didn't think that question would be asked.

The Bills' no-huddle offense captured the imagination of many football fans who loved fast, schoolyard football. The idea to use the no-huddle offense started in 1989 against Houston when the Bills scored twice to win on no-huddle drives. Offensive coordinator Ted Marchibroda thought, *If it worked at the end of the half and at the end of the game, why not use it regularly?* That idea took hold in their 12th game of the 1990 season, when Buffalo jumped out to a 24–0 lead in the first quarter. The no-huddle limited the defense's ability to confuse the offense. Coordinators like Belichick couldn't walk eight players up to the line of scrimmage with some dropping into coverage and others rushing the passer. Teams had to play safer defenses to prevent the big play, and limited substitution often left opponents exhausted.

The cover of Belichick's game plan had a caricature of a Giants player, wearing a large helmet, with his butt showing, urinating on a Bills helmet. It captured the Giants spirit going into the game—they wanted to ruin what many thought was already a predetermined Bills parade. In fact, the Bills' weekly itinerary called for a celebration at the team hotel at midnight on Sunday, January 27, 1991 into Monday, January 28, 1991. Belichick also wanted the players to laugh before diving into the 63 pages of technical football. To lighten the mood, players also started making lookalike comparisons, jokingly comparing LT to singer Dionne Warwick. Players placed this caricature in their lockers and throughout their dressing room.

By the end of the week, though, the Giants were drastically more serious than when they arrived on the plane from San Francisco. Worried about Jumbo Elliott's temper—who was assigned to block Bills All-Pro defensive end Bruce Smith—Parcells told Taylor on the bus to Friday's practice to pick a fight with Elliott so he could prove a point.

In his book *Inside the Helmet*, Michael Strahan wrote about Elliott's personality and the fight. "The thing about Jumbo was, if you beat him on a pass rush in practice you better watch your eyes, your throat, your head, and your ankles or else he'll get you…. Jumbo was just plain vindictive. He made you want to spit in his face damn near every practice. He was always slipping his fingers under my face mask, into my eyes, or punching my throat."

After Taylor beat him the first time, Elliott called him nothing but a speed rusher. The next time he said something far more offensive. "Yeah, well you're nothing but a fucking crackhead," Elliott said to Taylor.

Elliott was seeing red. Practice was stopped and the two had to be separated as Elliott continued to attack Taylor. Parcells went up to Elliott and told him that Taylor was just worried about how Elliott would handle a physical Bruce Smith in the Super Bowl. Jumbo got the point and forgave Taylor. All was well in Giantsville.

Pepper Johnson, who could have been a stand-up comedian, was the emcee of the Giants' festivities on the plane from San Francisco to Tampa. He used his drums to play conga music throughout the flight, with teammates dancing on each side of the aisle. William Roberts, a 6'7", 295-pound offensive tackle, Mark Collins, and Jumbo Elliott, to everyone's surprise, given the enormity of the 6'7", 308-pound offensive lineman, were dancing in one aisle. On the other side were Everson Walls, Reyna Thompson, Carl Banks, and Johnnie Cooks. Even Bill Parcells returned at one point to join the dancing festivities.

"By far the most impressive dancer, though, was William Roberts," Carthon remembers. "I don't think I ever saw a big man that could move so well. It was almost like watching Michael Jackson, the way he did the moonwalk. He once knocked down a lineman, guard, and safety all on one play.

"William was also one of the great pranksters on the team. He used to scare guys by telling them Parcells wanted to speak with them and then laugh in the back of the locker room when they would sit there all nervous, waiting for Coach."

Few players remember that President George H.W. Bush called Parcells during the flight and asked him if the Giants wanted to play or cancel the

Super Bowl. Parcells asked his players and they responded with unanimity about their desire to play. They joked with a ghostly sense of humor that if Tampa Stadium was destroyed, they would all have their hometown high school stadiums named in their honor. A lot of the players felt it was their duty to play the games because there was nothing else they could do and they realized football was an ideal distraction for an American public focused on war.

Twenty agencies, including the FBI, Customs, and anti-terrorist forces, coordinated security plans for Super Bowl XXV. The Giants needed to display parking passes on the front of their cars, since civilian cars were forbidden from approaching the parking garage closest to the stadium. Leonard Marshall and his father were detained outside the Giants locker room until coaches verified that he was in fact a member of the Giants. The all-encompassing security at the Super Bowl had two primary goals: limit access to the stadium and allow fans to have as few items as possible. No portable radios, headsets, televisions, or camcorders were allowed inside Tampa Stadium. Everything that was brought into the stadium had to be X-rayed. Tampa safety director Mike Smith was the most popular interview leading up the Super Bowl.

As an extra precaution, the FBI nixed the traditional Goodyear Blimp from taking aerial pictures of the game. A six-inch fence was erected around the stadium and the restricted air space was limited to within half a mile of Tampa Stadium. Fans couldn't even bring cameras into the stadium. A group of 2,000 proud parents learned this lesson when they arrived to take pictures of their children rehearsing for the halftime show and were told to stop.

Elliott, Howard, and linebacker Steve DeOssie somehow found fireworks and decided to set them off on the beach at the Giants hotel. The imagery of two linemen over 300 pounds and a linebacker who was about 270 pounds launching fireworks is something that Howard still laughs at to this day. Hotel security, though, didn't think it was so amusing. When they heard the sounds, they thought it might be a terrorist attack. All of a sudden police cars raced to the beach and started questioning the players.

"It was great," Howard remembers. "We were just a bunch of dudes having some fun. It was totally carefree. And the next thing we know, we are being investigated. It was quite obvious who we were after they pulled up in our cruisers."

Aside from the war, there were other tragedies clouding the game. Bills defensive lineman Leon Seals' mother was in a coma. She had worked three jobs to provide shelter and food for her family. Seals, like many players who grew up in a single-parent home, lauded his mother for being a survivor and for her willingness to stand up for what was right. He remembered being elbowed in the eye during a high school football game. His mother stepped onto the field to inform the coach that she was taking him to the hospital. She neither cared that parents weren't allowed on the field nor that her appearance might violate some rule. She knew that her son needed to go to the hospital and that was that.

Bills safety Leonard Smith empathized with Seals. His own father had died two months earlier. He admitted the difficulty of remaining focused on football after losing a family member or having one who is very sick. But Seals admitted football could be a welcome distraction, especially when you have teammates willing to rally around you when you are going through a difficult time.

Media Day is generally a time for the players and the media to have fun with each other. They players can try their hand at comedy and the media will write about it—after all, with seven days to report on one game, there are only so many angles that you can cover. Reporters often fill notebooks with the life stories of backup quarterbacks.

Offensive line coach Fred Hoaglin kept his promise to take his offensive linemen out for a steak dinner if the Giants made the Super Bowl. Hoaglin joked that the dinner probably cost him about $2,000, since many of his linemen ate two or three steaks. Mark Collins discussed how he could have played baseball and his similarities to Rickey Henderson, because he could hit, run, and steal a lot of bases. Matt Cavanaugh, the Giants backup who had replaced

Hostetler for a brief series during the NFC championship, joked that when he overthrew his intended target by about 10 yards on his only pass, he was unleashing all his energy from not throwing the ball all season.

Leonard Marshall, who shared agent Peter Johnson with Joe Montana, called Johnson to offer some encouraging words to Montana. Marshall admitted that if you get to the show and don't win, it can be what people remember. He wanted to see veteran players like Johnnie Cooks and Larry McGrew, two Giants guys who had never won a Super Bowl, earn rings. Marshall barely slept that week, or so he said, because he was dreaming of strip-sacking Jim Kelly and running the loose ball in for a touchdown with the Giants leading by three points toward the end of the fourth quarter.

Belichick's caricature of the Giants player urinating on the Bills helmet helped enforce a narrative that Giants coaches wanted their players to believe, about the Bills' arrogance and their expectation of a championship. He told them that Thurman Thomas fit himself for a Super Bowl ring four days before the game. Players also witnessed firsthand the Bills violating curfew by partying throughout the week.

"The thing about Thomas was a complete ploy by Parcells," Bills linebacker Cornelius Bennett said. "We all had to get measured for Super Bowl rings that week because it was the only time the team was together. But I give Parcells a lot of credit because it was a great motivational technique for his team. That is kind of what coaches do. The story is so improbable because I rode the bus with Thurman and he was just thinking about winning the game. He didn't even know about all the Super Bowl celebration stuff."

When the Giants arrived in Tampa the next morning, few expected them to be there. Signs everywhere indicated that a Bills-49ers matchup was a forgone conclusion. San Francisco 49ers paraphernalia decorated the Giants' hotel. Some hotel staff had missed the finale in the NFC Championship Game the night before and expected the 49ers to check in. The hotel concierge expected Joe Montana and Jerry Rice, yet found Jeff Hostetler and Stephen

Baker. The 49ers had even chosen their lunch and dinner menus at the hotel for the week prior to the Super Bowl.

"It had lobsters and steaks and all this fancy food," Bob Kratch said. "One of the first things we did was change the menu. We were a blue-collar team. We didn't have players like Montana and Rice. We were happy with hamburgers and french fries."

Kratch had a point. Other than LT, the Giants didn't have any future Hall of Famers. The Giants sensed a cool arrogance among the Bills players and Parcells wanted the Bills to believe their own press clippings. He told his players to talk up the Bills or "blow smoke up their ass," in the hope that the Bills would forget that both teams finished the regular season 13–3. When the two teams met in the regular season, the Bills narrowly defeated the Giants 17–13. But it was the game in which quarterback Phil Simms broke his foot, landing him on injured reserve for the rest of the season.

"He didn't want us to give them any bulletin board material," Walls said.

Defensively, players discussed how difficult it was to stop the no-huddle offense. Some points were legitimate, others could be considered puffery. Veteran safety Dave Duerson joked that the Giants needed their track shoes to stop the Bills offense. Banks, in his iconic wide-rimmed sunglasses, said that if the Bills were a basketball team it would be like trying to cover five Michael Jordans. Linebacker Pepper Johnson worried about stopping the run and Marshall looked forward to the challenge of playing against the no-huddle offense. Players insisted that the Bills offense was unlike anything they had ever seen before and few players mentioned any flaws.

Early that week, Parcells realized that time of possession was the crucial statistic. If the Bills and Giants had the ball the same amount of time, the Bills were going to outscore them, pure and simple.

Before Belichick introduced the game plan to his players, he made them watch the full television broadcasts of the Bills' two playoff victories over the Los Angeles Raiders and Miami Dolphins. Usually, players watch sliced-up film divided into sections based on different situations. They might watch a group of second-and-10 plays together, third-and-long, and so on. The problem with that approach against the Bills was that it didn't give players a sense of how quick the Bills' no-huddle offense was. Unlike other teams that ran the hurry-up—where the offensive coordinator might relay two or three plays in at a time—Jim Kelly did not receive any direction from the sideline. Jim Kelly made his own calls. Players needed to be ready.

"I really think it was a brilliant move because it caused us to say, 'Holy shit, this is a fast offense,'" said Giants cornerback Mark Collins.

Belichick gave his team the game plan and offered a simple directive that at first seemed outlandish to his players but then made sense. He told the Giants that in order for them to win, Thurman Thomas needed to rush for more than 100 yards. For many of the Giants' defensive players, holding a running back to under 100 yards was a point of pride. The Giants also had one of the best run defenses in football that year and were used to shutting down opponents' running backs. Belichick, however, realized that if Thomas ran for 100 yards it would accomplish two things: slow down the game and the Bills passing attack.

When he finally asked his players if they were with him, they begrudgingly said yes. The game plan revolved heavily on where Thomas was lined up before the snap. The Giants utilized three defenses to stop the Bills: big nickel, little nickel, and dime defense. The main difference between the two nickel defenses was that in big nickel Pepper Johnson played at his normal linebacker spot and in little nickel he lined up at defensive end. The dime defense added a sixth defensive back to the mix, usually Greg Jackson.

New York ran what they termed their "regular people" defense—when the offense ran its standard formation with two running backs, two wide receivers, and a tight end. The Bills often ran this formation on first down and were likely to run with Thomas lined up behind Kelly. Marshall ran a hawk blitz, a run-pass blitz where he smashed the guard into the tackle to eliminate an inside hole. It would force Thomas outside, where he had no help. On the sidelines, Belichick made the hawk motion numerous times. If the Bills tried to throw with regular people, the Giants funneled the receivers to the inside with a clamp on Andre Reed to prevent him from getting off the line of scrimmage. LT, much to the shock of Bills center Kent Hull, lined up over him and rushed with Howard to the inside as Marshall looped around from his outside position to be in Kelly's face making him throw quicker than he wanted to.

The Giants, however, realized that while these blitzes might be helpful, they failed to address the critical issue of how to stop Thurman Thomas in the passing game. The Giants understood that the Bills scored 95 points combined in their two playoff games largely because of the slip screen to Thomas who, if not checked at the line of scrimmage, could escape and catch a two-yard pass that allowed him to have forward momentum to run. Therefore, Marshall or Johnson checked Thomas before rushing Kelly so Thomas failed to have a clean release.

"I made sure to knock the shit out of Thurman every time because that was my first responsibility," Marshall remembers.

He wanted Thomas to arc release so he was forced out of his pattern and needed to make an arc to get back into it. Marshall's biggest fear was for Thomas to flat release so he had momentum in his route. If he caught the ball, Marshall wanted him in the closed position in the middle of the field so Kelly couldn't dump the ball over his head and he was in an easier position to make the tackle. Marshall also knew he had more help in the middle of the field.

The Giants' decision on who to send on a blitz was also predicated on where Thomas lined up. If Thomas lined up on the side with the tight end, Taylor rushed. If Thomas lined up on the opposite side, then the defensive lineman or linebacker who was closest to Thomas—either Marshall, Pepper Johnson, or LT—needed to "butch the back," or hit him as hard as he could. When the Bills switched back to regular people with the quarterback under center, Giants players would scream "Chicago" to denote the likelihood of a run. "Idaho" was their dummy call to prevent the Bills from thinking that the Giants had picked up on what they were doing.

The Giants were also worried about the crossing patterns of Andre Reed. The Bills particularly liked to call the dig H-Reed, where Reed came across the middle and Thomas tried to run a slip screen either outside or inside of the hashes, depending on how Reed broke his route. If Reed broke toward the sideline, Thomas would go over the middle. The reverse was true as well. It was a route that the Giants were determined to stop by hitting Reed as much as possible. Almost every time Reed came across the middle, either Carl Banks or Pepper Johnson whacked him, causing him to either drop the pass or stop him for no gain after the catch.

"We were going to let you catch the ball, but the punishment would be severe," Everson Walls said.

Afterward, Reed indeed admitted that he had never been hit so hard in his life. "It felt like there were more than 11 guys on the field," he said.

Stopping Reed without your two best corners was considered unthinkable. It was one of Belichick's finest achievements. Special teams ace Reyna Thompson, the Giants' fourth best cover corner who struggled in tight coverage, lined up against Reed in the slot. His assignment was simply to force Reed to the middle where Banks occupied the zone in little nickel and Johnson did the same in big nickel. Belichick astutely realized that he could use his worst corner to fill this role, utilizing his better corners on the Bills' other receivers. In dime situations, the Giants would use Jackson, a defensive back, to cover the tight end. Belichick also needed to substitute creatively and quickly. Carl Banks, who was responsible for making the Giants' calls in the front seven, had a checklist after watching this tape with three critical elements on it.

1. Make sure that every defender is lined up against someone on offense and that no one roams free.

2. Have the defensive signals called quickly.

3. Get the defensive lineman in position. If he remains standing, it is all over.

One unconventional method that the Giants used to slow down the Bills offense was to have "designated crampees," players who faked cramps when they were supposed to run off the field. If the sideline wanted a player to fake a cramp, one of the coaches pointed his fingers to make a gun-like signal. Often, a Giants trainer helped the faker off the field. The strategy essentially gave New York a free timeout. The left end was responsible for reading the injury situation and alerting the coaches as to who might be faking an injury. Generally, it would either be Fox, Eric Dorsey, or John Washington who would pretend to cramp.

They would also kick the ball away from the line of scrimmage on several occasions. Overall, the Giants would keep the substitutions simple. When they switched from big nickel to little nickel they replaced rookie nose tackle Mike Fox, who played well against the run, with Gary Reasons. The Bills rated Reasons as the Giants' best coverage linebacker and were particularly impressed with his ability to cover tight ends and running backs. The Giants also wanted him in the middle of the field because of how well he could read a quarterback's eyes.

Two of the plays the Giants worried about most were the shovel pass and the i-trap.

In the shovel-pass formation, the Bills aligned in a three wide receiver set with Thomas offset right, indicating that the play was a pass. When Thomas lined up under center, New York knew that he would run. But if he was offset left, right, or next to Kelly in the shotgun, then they expected a pass. Belichick told Marshall that he wanted him to be a "bastard" in their offensive backfield and be physical with the Bills' 325-pound right tackle, Howard Ballard. This advice was especially critical on the shovel because Marshall needed to seal Ballard with a three technique. This meant that he had to prevent Ballard from making an angle block to allow Thomas outside. On the second part of the play, the right guard swept around to the other side of the field and Thomas moved several yards from Kelly to catch the shovel pass. The Giants' scout team ran this play numerous times, with Dave Meggett imitating Thomas. In fact, Meggett ran this play so well in practice that the Giants decided to make it part of their offensive game plan.

The Giants simply knew they had to keep Thomas from getting to the outside because of his punishing speed.

"We knew he ran a 4.3 while our linebackers ran a 4.5 or 4.6," Marshall said.

At the beginning of practice on Thursday, the Giants scout team ran the shovel-pass play six straight times with different defenses, all of them variations of the nickel with an even front (two defensive linemen, four linebackers). The goal was to have at least four defenders at the line-of-scrimmage attack.

The fourth defense was a dime package (six defensive backs) that the Giants would use in long passing situations with Howard, Marshall, and Johnson on the line of scrimmage as Taylor and Banks were in the backfield. This alignment was given the title of "joker" because of how it confused the offense, since the linemen and linebackers blitzed while safety Greg Jackson played like a linebacker in the middle of the field. The Giants would often use this formation when the Bills used an empty backfield or played with four wide receivers. The Giants also had dummy calls such as "Reno" and "Vegas" to make the Bills think they were calling something different against the same formation.

What made Belichick's game plan special was that even though it confused the Bills, it did not confuse his own players. "We were in four basic defenses," said Walls. "All the players knew what they had to do. We did little things to confuse them, but there was really nothing exotic."

The Giants ran the game plan until they knew it down pat. But the question remained: would it work?

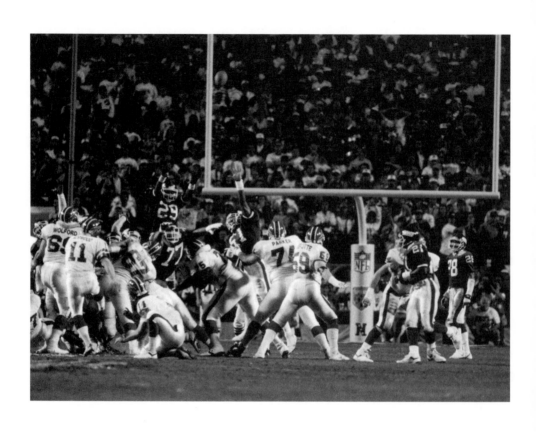

Super

MANY OF THE PLAYERS IN SUPER BOWL XXV still think about hearing their names called in the pregame introductions and seeing almost every fan in the stadium waving small American flags, many of them with tears in their eyes. It still gives Jeff Hostetler the chills when he thinks about it. For many, it was the first time the U.S. had been involved in a war in their lifetime. Others were too young to remember Vietnam. That inexperience led to a general fear over what-if scenarios. Just about everybody in the press box was crying when Whitney Houston sang the national anthem.

Marshall joked that it was a good omen for the Giants that she sang in their direction. "It gave us an advantage," he said sarcastically.

The Bills' Darryl Talley thinks it made players realize that the game was something special. Other players tried ignore all that was around them and focus on the task ahead. "I think players would be lying if they told you that they didn't get emotional during the opening ceremonies," Talley said.

ESPN producer Tim Nickles, who was part of a marine helicopter squadron at the time, was stationed in Saudi Arabia and couldn't get the signal on the Armed Forces Radio Network. He missed the first quarter and a half. It was upsetting, to say the least, for an avid Bills fan who grew up in Jamestown, New York, about an hour south of Buffalo. The game started at 2:30 AM in the Middle East and Nickles had to be to work by 7:00 AM the next morning.

"I knew I was going to be a little tired, to say the least," Nickles said.

Nickles finally received the audio feed of the ABC broadcast in the second quarter before retreating to his tent to listen to the second half on Westwood One with his old-fashioned Sony Walkman. With his limited technology, Nickles felt he was stepping back 20 years in time. Because it was his team playing, he couldn't watch the game in the company of other people; he needed to be alone. He had a slight out-of-body experience, thinking that it was cool to listen to the Super Bowl almost 4,000 miles from Tampa. For Nickles and his squadron, football was an escape from the daily grind of the military and also provided fodder for the troops to razz one another. He'd soon get plenty of it from Giants fans.

Giants captains Carl Banks and LT took the field, along with Steve Tasker Andre Reed, Darryl Talley, Kent Hull, and Mark Kelso for the opening coin toss by former NFL commissioner Pete Rozelle.

Parcells understood that the Giants relied on a strong defense and he made sure to keep it that way during his eight years in New York. When the Giants won the Super Bowl in 1986, they were dominating opponents—blowing out the 49ers 49–3 in the NFC playoffs and making the Denver Broncos look like a JV team in the second half of Super Bowl XXI as they scored only ten points. Taylor had 20.5 sacks and was named NFL Defensive Player of the Year. Marshall recorded 12.5 sacks and had three fumble recoveries.

Yet Parcells knew that the Giants had an aging defense with Jim Burt, George Martin, and Harry Carson all on the decline. To the surprise of everyone, he focused on revamping his defense before the 1986 draft, as Parcells selected six defensive players in the early rounds who played crucial roles on the 1990 team, including Eric Dorsey, Mark Collins, John Washington, Pepper Johnson, and Erik Howard. Dorsey, Howard, and Washington made up three-fifths of the Giants defensive line. All saw limited action in '86, but the experience showed its value in 1990.

The Giants also were a strong running team and needed to rebuild their offensive line. Center Bart Oates was the only Giants offensive lineman to start on the 1986 and 1990 teams. Teammates jokingly referred to Oates as "Mr. Counselor" because he was in the process of earning his law degree while he played. They also teased him that center was the easiest position on the offensive line because they have protection on both sides.

Parcells drafted right tackle Doug Riesenberg in 1987 along with starter Eric Moore and Jumbo Elliott in 1988. William Roberts, whom the Giants drafted in 1984, was also a starter on the Giants' 1990 team. New York also added Mark Ingram and Stephen Baker, who became their two main wide receivers in 1990. The Giants' strong drafting in the late '80s materialized in 1990 with a top-notch running game and defense.

"The change in the offensive line from the '86 to the '90 team was we went from a smaller, nimble offensive line to one of the biggest offensive lines in the league," said Bavaro. "I also think we were more athletic than in 1986. Bart Oates, who was one of the biggest guys on the '86 team, seemed very small with all the big linemen we had in '90. Riesenberg was probably one of my best friends on the team. We both had similar personalities: hardworking guys who didn't talk a lot and we worked well together on a lot of combo blocks."

Parcells could play the type of football that he loved, knowing that teams who scored the highest number of points were not always the ones to win the Super Bowl. Good defense and a strong running game were far more important. The three teams who scored the most points in one season all failed to win a Super Bowl—the '98 Minnesota Vikings, the '83 Washington Redskins, and later, the '07 Patriots.

The Giants offensive line was determined to overpower the Bills. From the outset, the Giants' game plan was clear—particularly when offensive coordinator Ron Erhardt screamed "three tight ends" to Hostetler as the Giants offense ran onto the field for their first possession. When Giants players are asked about the game plan, inevitably they use phrases like "shove it down their throat" and "keep them down on the ground" to describe their goal.

"We knew that the Bills were not an overpowering team, but a group that was based on speed and the big play," said Giants tight end Howard Cross. "Their defense was used to sitting back and rushing the passer because they often had big leads with their K-gun offense. If we could run the ball effectively, we knew it would make them uncomfortable."

To do so, they had to contain Bruce Smith, which sometimes required double-teams from Cross and Elliott. Cross, though, preferred to leave Elliott alone because he was so big and dominating. They also had to worry about Cornelius Bennett, whose pass rush was devastating.

The results for the Giants in the first half were mixed. Kicker Matt Bahr made the tackle on the opening kickoff, to the amusement of many Giants players who had seen him do the same thing before. That tackle makes for a great trivia question to stump a friend: Who had the first tackle in Super Bowl XXV?

"Matt was crazy. He had to be in the thick of the action and make a tackle with his one-ring face mask, being the smallest guy on the field," said Cross, who played on special teams with Bahr. "We kept thinking, *This guy is going to get killed if he keeps doing this and we are probably going to have to carry him off the field.*"

The Giants, though, started to implement their game plan immediately. Maurice Carthon ran for a first down after two straight runs. Dave Meggett added another first down run later in the drive. At the outset of the play, he fell down, but he quickly leaped to his feet to gain 10 yards. Early on, Hostetler demonstrated the extra dimension he gave the Giants over Phil Simms—his mobility—when he completed a rollout to Howard Cross that was good for another 13 yards.

"On these rollouts, the Bills apparently didn't do their homework because they kept trying to put more players in the box to pressure the quarterback. All that did, though, was create more space for me in the open field to catch the ball," said Cross, who had been playing with a broken wrist all season.

Unfortunately, it was also apparent that Hostetler didn't have the arm of Phil Simms when he overthrew Mark Bavaro on a seam route—at the 10. Bavaro was open, and the pass should have been a touchdown. The seam route was what Bavaro, who had never seen the route before the Giants drafted him, called the Giants' "bread and butter," with two receivers running long routes trying to split the deep safety. Simms threw the route as well as anyone, and Hostetler, who had practiced numerous times, wasn't as good as Simms. On this particular play, the two had a miscommunication. Bavaro thought he was supposed to stop at about the 10, and Hostetler thought he would keep running. (The debate was a source of tension at halftime between Bavaro and the coaches, as he reminded the coaches that he was taught to stop in the open area.)

Hostetler completed a third-down pass to Mark Ingram on third-and-7 at the Bills 31 to gain 16 yards. After Hostetler missed Ingram in the end zone several plays later, Matt Bahr kicked a field goal to give the Giants a 3–0 lead. ESPN statistics guru Russell Baxter—who has taped and rewatched thousands of NFL games and can talk extemporaneously about specific plays in a Super Bowl—told a friend to look at the scoreboard.

"Yeah, 3–0," he responded.

Baxter shot back, "There is [7:14] remaining. The Giants just took [almost] 10 minutes off the clock."

When James Lofton caught a 61-yard pass on the Bills' ensuing possession after a Perry Williams tip, the Giants defense didn't panic.

"We knew they got one on us, but we were determined not to let it happen again," said Walls, whose hustle to push Lofton out of bounds saved a touchdown. The Giants had kept it together, and Buffalo came away with only a field goal.

The Giants played just two defenses in the red zone—either their regular 3-4 or Red Two Dallas, where they double-teamed Thurman Thomas and Andre Reed. The latter was effective on third-and-goal from the 5 with Kelly in the shotgun. Buffalo called a double seam, H-reed, signaling that Reed was on the weak side. Reed, tight end Keith McKeller, and Al Edwards were all supposed to run seam routes straight up the field to make room for Thomas, who was running a screen. Walls and Guyton double-teamed Thomas while Collins and Banks covered Reed. When Kelly threw to Thomas, Guyton and Walls hit him at the same time, sending the ball careening into the air and leading Walls to catch a would-be interception on the sideline.

The Bills were starting to look like the same Bills that demolished the Dolphins and Raiders in their two playoff games when Kelly led them on an 80-yard, four-and-a-half-minute touchdown drive early in the second quarter. Kelly seemed in sync with Reed, completing four passes, three of them for nine or more yards. With the Bills inside the 20 and a worn-out Giants defense, Marshall purposely committed a personal foul penalty in order to give the Giants a chance to substitute. Two seconds after Kelly completed a five-yard pass to McKeller, Marshall pushed him to the ground.

Said Dierdorf from the broadcast booth, "It is critical for Leonard to hold up on that play. That is flagrant."

Added Marshall, "We needed new personnel on the field. Kelly was finding ways to connect with Reed, even when we blitzed. Earlier in the drive, he hit Reed for a 20-yard pass even though we had the perfect blitz on, and I hit him right as he threw the ball. Thurman was also running well.

"I also wanted to send Kelly a message that he was going to get hit. It was something that didn't happen in the Bills' two playoff games. Thirdly, there was some payback from when he ignored my boy Perry [Williams] and [me] after seeing him at a bar earlier that week.

"When Don Smith ran for the touchdown, we weren't that upset. They had earned it. It wasn't like we gave them anything. They made some creative adjustments and we had a lot of faith that our offense could get us back in the game."

It would take a bit longer for his faith to materialize. The Bills' pressure on the Giants offense increased as corner Kirby Jackson hit Hostetler on a safety blitz. Nose tackle Leon Seals also took advantage of the Giants double-teaming Bruce Smith. The Bills astutely moved Smith to the other side of the line so

Elliott, responsible for protecting the quarterback's blind side, wouldn't block him. Pressuring Hostetler was easier from the right side of the Giants' offensive line than the left side.

On third down Smith made a big inside move, occupying right guard Moore and Riesenberg. Seals looped around to the outside and leveled Hostetler with the full force of his body. Hostetler was on the ground for five seconds. Trainer Ronnie Barnes put smelling salts under Hostetler's nose, but the quarterback could hardly smell them—something that shocked his teammate Stephen Baker, who thought the odor was maybe the strongest he had ever experienced.

"The trainers looked at me and I looked at them and we didn't have anything to say, but we were all thinking, *Something is really wrong here*," said Baker.

Added Bennett, "I don't know how he got up from that play. When Leon made the hit, I thought Hostetler would be out for the game. We didn't want him to get hurt, but you just said to yourself, *There is no way he is getting up*."

Giants fans were nervous when they heard Al Michaels announce before a commercial that Matt Cavanaugh was the Giants' backup and the emergency quarterback was Ingram, their best wide receiver. Meggett could also take a few snaps in desperation. Giants fans cringed, remembering how Cavanaugh overthrew his intended target by 10 yards in the NFC Championship Game. Hostetler, thankfully, soon started throwing warm-up passes and seemed to be all right.

The score 10–3, the Giants defense was determined to stop the Bills on their next possession. A 17–3 deficit was too much for the Giants offense to overcome, particularly with Hostetler's return anything but a certainty. On the Bills' first play, Thomas ran 14 yards for a first down—but it might have been 30 yards had Walls not grabbed Thomas by the ankles from behind. It was his second clutch tackle of the game.

"For an old vet, Walls played really well. He made a lot of big tackles that made you think about what would have happened if he didn't make the play," Parcells said.

On the Bills' next play, Thomas ran four yards to set up second-and-6. The Bills returned to the air when Kelly threw a 20-yard pass to Reed. Happily for New York, it was ruled incomplete after Myron Guyton hit the receiver as soon as he touched the ball. A Giants offsides penalty set up a third-and-1 play, but Reed dropped the pass over the middle as he was about to receive a major hit from Pepper Johnson.

Said then Bills GM and current Colts president Bill Polian, "There were a few plays in the game that we should have made, and if we make those plays, we win the game. This play was one of them. I don't care what anyone says about Andre Reed, he is definitely a Hall of Fame wide receiver, and this is the play he normally makes."

Interestingly, Polian and Marv Levy insist they didn't know that the Bills were favored. "I never once looked at the spread," Levy said.

The Giants, regaining possession and starting a new series, were pinned back at their own seven. And their luck wasn't getting any better. On their second play of the series, an Ottis Anderson run almost gave the Giants a first down—only it was called back by a Bart Oates holding penalty. Hostetler dropped back on second down, yet Ottis Anderson never moved toward the line of scrimmage to pick up Bruce Smith's blitz and Hostetler's left foot collided with Anderson's right foot.

"The toughest thing about Bruce Smith was he was slick, like LT. You would think you had him blocked, and he would somehow escape," said Bill Belichick.

Hostetler stumbled into the end zone, where Smith sacked him for a safety to make it 12–3 Bills. Dierdorf astutely noted that the Giants were fortunate to only lose two points. The replay explained why. Before Smith tackled Hostetler, he grabbed his wrist to strip the ball, thinking about a touchdown. Hostetler astutely sensed Smith's hand and corralled the ball into his chest to prevent a fumble.

"We could have easily been down 14 points. Jeff probably made the most intelligent play of the game," Parcells said.

Added Bennett, "We did not think the game was over. Coach Levy would always tell us, 'Where would you rather be than right here, right now?' It was a tired cliché, but it taught us to live in the moment. We couldn't wait to get up and play on Sunday. I think that attitude is what united the two teams."

So while the Bills celebrated with Smith continuously putting his hands together for about five seconds, the Giants quietly enjoyed their own victory. Still, many felt it was only matter of time before the Bills offense exploded.

Myron Guyton forced Reed to drop another pass on first down with a big hit. The Bills had recognized Kelly's difficulty in throwing crossing routes to Reed by late in the first quarter. They now tried to have him run up the field instead. But Guyton was proving to be just as punishing as Johnson and Banks.

"You really couldn't have asked Myron to play any better than he did," Walls said. "He really did everything we asked and a lot more."

Early on, the Giants offense had run Meggett a lot because they thought that the Bills offense had a lot of great athletes but also a tendency to gamble— sometimes knifing inside one too many gaps.

"We were an undersized group so we knew that we had to take chances," Bennett said.

They thought Meggett was the best running back to take advantage of this flaw, but the Bills had found ways to stop him. So they started to run Anderson more. Even so, the Giants went three-and-out on their second straight possession in the second quarter.

One of the issues the Giants were having was that Hostetler was rolling toward the faster Bennett and away from Smith, causing him to receive more pressure. "Sometimes, if you try to roll away from a pass rusher, he becomes more destructive," said Oates. "If you roll toward him, though, you neutralize him because he has to respect that the quarterback might run or take off."

Buffalo started another drive that could have put the Giants away when Thomas gained 40 yards on the Bills' first four plays, with two runs and two passes. Offensive lineman Howard Ballard started to force Marshall to the inside so he couldn't hit Thomas before the runner started his route.

"You really had to hit Thomas. Ballard did a good job on that drive of only allowing me to nick Thomas. It wasn't enough to stop him," said Marshall.

On second-and-2 at the Giants 44, Kelly tried to throw the same deep pass that he completed to Lofton in the first quarter, but Kelly underthrew him; Perry Williams and Walls knocked the ball away. The Bills made another mistake on the next play when Will Wolford was called for a false start to force a third-and-7 instead of third-and-2. Those five yards proved critical on the next down, when Andre Reed caught a five-yard pass and Banks immediately tackled him, leaving him two yards short of the first down.

When the Giants took over with 3:49 remaining, their offense had been anemic. Some Giants players were not even thinking about scoring. They just hoped that the offense could keep possession with a couple of first downs so they could keep the score 12–3 going into the half.

"At that point our attitude was, *let's just go out there and get a first down,*" Kratch said. "It wasn't any more complicated than that."

Anderson had only rushed for 21 yards to this point. The Giants started running at Smith instead of away from him. Because if Smith had a weakness, it was his ability to stop the run. The Giants kept running Anderson. Even if he didn't gain a lot of yards, his power would at least wear out the Bills' defense. On the Giants' first play, Hostetler hit Bavaro for a modest six-yard gain. Anderson completed his first long run of 18 yards to the Giants 37—giving the Giants a first down.

"That's kind of the way Ottis was," Cross said. "He would run for three or four yards and then break out for 10 or more yards. Most of his running was between the tackles, so that made him especially tough because he would hit you on every play. And if we blocked the linebackers, you would get O.J. on a safety, which was a weight differential of about 30 pounds."

The Giants had their first first down in more than a quarter, and with that accomplishment out of the way, the Giants could worry about scoring. Hostetler made a play-action fake to Meggett and hit Ingram along the side-lines for an 18-yard gain to the Bills 41. Meggett then made a slashing run for 17 yards to the Giants 24. On a critical third-and-7 from the 21, Hostetler continued to throw the ball poorly. His pass seemed headed for the ground, but Cross dove and somehow made the first-down catch.

"If he throws it correctly he has a touchdown," Dierdorf said.

Bennett once again showed why the Giants needed to roll toward Smith's side when he batted down another pass. Hostetler missed another chance for a touchdown when he underthrew Baker in the middle of the end zone. Finally, the Giants called their signature red-zone play. Baker, who was 5'8" and fast enough for his teammates to joke that if you played a game of tag against him you would never find him, ran a flag route straight at the Bills cornerback, faking inside and moving outside, as Hostetler finally made a good pass to hit Baker in the corner of the end zone.

"Stephen was great to have on our team, because whenever things got serious he knew how to lighten the mood by playing a practical joke," Carthon said. He was also, it appeared, valuable in the clutch.

"We were pretty confident going into the half because we knew that they had given us our best shot and missed a lot of opportunities. We knew we could play a lot better," Marshall said.

If there was ever a patriotic Super Bowl, this might have been it. It was on display as the New Kids on the Block performed at halftime, featuring contest-winner Seth Horton dressed in a football uniform holding a helmet and singing "You Are My Hero," dedicated to U.S. troops in the Persian Gulf. Children of parents serving in the Gulf War representing each of the 50 states were allowed to stand on the field as President George H.W. Bush paid thanks to our troops in a prerecorded message that he completed earlier in the week. The halftime show was the NFL at its finest—exciting football mixed with a magical sense of patriotism.

Tampa Stadium was decorated throughout with red, white, and blue. "God Bless America" played in the background. The New Kids on the Block, during their 20 minutes of airtime, were on the field longer than the Bills offense, which, except for Kelly and the offense kneeling down on the last play of the half, sat on the bench for over an hour, from the 3:49 mark of the second quarter to the 5:31 mark of the third quarter.

Baxter still marvels at the Giants' 9:29 drive to open the third quarter—then the longest in Super Bowl history (Eli Manning's Giants in Super Bowl XLII now hold that distinction). Anderson still signs autographs because of it and the Bills certainly think about their missed tackles on third down. Heading into the drive, the Giants had already run 17 times, more attempts than Thomas would have in the entire game. Baxter, who charts rushing yards versus attempts, says there is an almost 10-point difference in predicting who wins when comparing the two statistics. The team that rushes for more yards will win almost 70 percent of the time and the team that has more attempts will win about 80 percent of the time.

"That is how you develop your play-action and wear the other team out. A lot of people think you need to throw to get back into a game, but running is far better. Many forget that when Joe Montana threw his famous touchdown pass to Dwight Clark, the 49ers ran the ball on most of the drive to set up the pass, because the Cowboys were using five and six defensive backs," said Baxter.

Baxter's research is applicable in this situation. The Giants rushed for approximately the same number of yards as the Bills, but they ran 14 more times. If the Bills made one major mistake, it was not running Thomas *more*, though he finished with 15 carries for 135 yards and nine yards per carry. Say the Bills ran him five more times. Additional time elapses and the Giants would have allocated more players to stop the run, opening up the Bills passing game. During the season, the Bills often played with the comfort of a lead, which allowed them the flexibility to blitz a lot. Now, in a tight game, they were in unfamiliar territory. As the game continued, the Bills' confidence waned as the Giants' psyche grew.

"If a team like the Bills is favored in a big game, they generally either blow out an opponent or lose a squeaker. They don't usually win a squeaker because in these types of games, the favorite usually becomes unnerved or uncomfortable," said Baxter.

The Bills' fatigue helps explain their careless tackling on two crucial third downs. The first example occurred on third-and-8 from the Giants 27, when Hostetler threw a three-yard pass to Meggett. Clifford Hicks missed Meggett low and Darryl Talley missed him high, and Meggett ran another eight yards for the first down. Interestingly enough, the Giants called few plays on the drive that required Hostetler to make tough throws, in spite of his struggles in the first half.

"I think the missed tackles mentally drained [the Bills] because you could tell they were thinking *we are not supposed to be out here right now* and they were thinking more about past plays than future plays," said Cross. "In games like the Super Bowl momentum plays such a big role, and once it starts rolling it is tough to stop."

The next two Giants plays were indicative of the Giants winning the battle up front. Meggett ran four yards to the left, and Anderson moved the pile three yards to gain five yards, setting up a third-and-1 at the Giants 47.

The Bills defense nearly collapsed when Smith almost gave up on the play after Elliott pushed him inside. Talley was sealed at the point of attack and Anderson galloped into Buffalo territory. Bills safety Mark Kelso had his arms around Anderson at the 35, but O.J. dragged him five more yards until he was wrestled down at the 30 for a 23-yard gain. Dierdorf jokingly asked if this was No. 34 or No. 24, referring to Thurman Thomas' number.

"[Anderson] was so much fun to watch run because of how he just hit people and kept on moving. If you ran into him, he was almost going to hurt you. Sometimes he would punch players from behind," Marshall says.

The Giants' running attack didn't stop there. On the next play, Carthon should have been tackled after two yards, but he gained three more as the Bills struggled to bring him down. The Giants had gained more than 120 yards to this point, averaging over 6 yards a carry. By comparison, no team all season had averaged more than 4.5 yards per carry in a game.

"I learned to run like that when I was playing in the USFL with Herschel Walker," said Carthon. "He always knew how to gain those extra yards, and I wanted to be just like him."

Nonetheless, the Bills still had a chance to stop the Giants at the 32 on third-and-13 after a Dave Meggett run was called back because of a hold. Hostetler threw Ingram a simple crossing route over the middle, which he caught about seven yards from the line of scrimmage. The Giants' first aim on the play was to get in field-goal range, because a 50-yarder was beyond Bahr's range.

"Hostetler really had two options on the play," Cross said. "He could either throw to Ingram over the middle, the safe route, or try and find Baker deep. But the Bills were determined to prevent the first down, so he had little choice but to throw to Ingram."

A 43-yard kick was more practical and the Giants accomplished their goal with Ingram's completion. But the Bills somehow forgot how to tackle. Kirby Jackson missed Ingram in the open field about six yards from the sticks. Talley tried to grab him by the neck after an eight-yard gain, but Ingram escaped. Kelso had a chance, two yards from the first down, but Ingram faked him out before lunging for a first down as corner James Williams held him in the air with his foot. The ball just crossed the 19-yard line—exactly where it needed to be for a first down.

Said Dierdorf, "Sometimes you will look back at a football game and say on that play it was won or lost. This might have been the play."

Years later, Giants fans rhetorically ask if there could be a more demoralizing play than that one. They know the answer. Five plays, four runs, and a pass later Anderson ran for a one-yard touchdown. He finished the drive with 37 yards, but it might as well have been 137 yards as far as the Bills were concerned. It took almost four and five guys to bring him down on every play. The

Giants offensive line had manhandled the Bills defense to the point where it appeared on some plays that the Bills' effort was minimal at best.

"All you have to do is look at the grass stains on Bruce Smith's ass and that tells you how much Jumbo dominated Bruce," Marshall said.

Added Bavaro, "I don't use the word 'dominating' much, but you could say Jumbo dominated Bruce in the Super Bowl."

On the other side of the line, Bavaro had neutralized Bennett, the Bills' second-best pass rusher, allowing the Giants to run to the right or left. Refreshed, the Giants forced the Bills to punt after just one first down, thanks to a sack from Leonard Marshall on third-and-18.

The Giants continued their strategy on the next possession, but the Bills stopped them after only one first down, when Anderson failed to convert on fourth-and-2 after running into Smith. Unfortunately, Smith came through blocked. Bavaro had moved upfield to block Talley and Elliott blocked a blitzer, leaving Smith free.

There were other plays that gave them more trouble. The Giants struggled with Sprint 34, a basic off tackle running play that allowed Thomas to run for a 31-yard touchdown at the beginning of the fourth quarter. All-Pro center Kent Hull made a superb block on nose tackle Erik Howard, pushing him four yards off the line of scrimmage by the time Thomas got to the point of attack.

What surprised the Giants was that, with Kelly in the shotgun, they expected a pass as opposed to a run. Still, linebacker Gary Reasons should have made the tackle. With the Giants' standard 2-4-5 little nickel defense, stopping the run was difficult because the Giants lacked the personnel required to handle the Bills' mammoth offensive line that had two players of over 300 pounds on their right side. The other issue was the little nickel defense had Reasons, a linebacker, in place of Mike Fox, a big defensive tackle. To say that this defense wasn't meant to stop the run was an understatement. But Belichick had chosen to play the percentages, thinking that Buffalo was still more likely to pass than run in this formation.

"We were exhausted and Belichick was upset on the sidelines because of how much Howard got exposed on that play by Hull. And we also realized that Reasons could have made the tackle," Marshall said. "After that touchdown, we were exhausted. We were just hoping that our offense could put something together," Marshall said. "It was a pretty humid night out there."

The offense remembered that it was the Giants defense who bailed them out in the second quarter by not allowing any more points when the Bills tried to build an insurmountable lead. Now it was their turn to help the defense. Pressure was mounting as the Bills offense, evidenced by the Thomas touchdown, could explode on any given play.

Finally, the combination of Anderson and Bavaro paid off. Many argue that if there had been a co-MVP in this game it should have been the Giants' offensive line because of how well they blocked. But a case could be also made for Bavaro. Bennett still claims that he was the best athlete on the field, and it wasn't Bavaro who shut him down, but rather the Giants' max protection.

"Blocking Bennett didn't feel that tough, because I really lined up against the best players in practice every day in Marshall, Taylor, and Banks. But Talley was just as formidable of an opponent because of his size and speed," Bavaro said. "The guy who gave me the most trouble that I often had to block was Reggie White. You would try to keep him away from the ball carrier, but it was very hard. You couldn't dominate him and you could never really say with White that you won the battle. A stalemate was what you were hoping for. As far as a linebacker, the best I had to block was Andre Tippett from the Patriots. Luckily, we didn't play them that much. I thought I was a good blocker, though I never considered myself to be a dominant blocker because in the NFC East we played against a lot of really good players."

Bavaro caught a 17-yard pass that gave the Giants a first down when they faced third-and-7. Normally, the Giants defense sat on the bench and rested when the offense was on the field. They would review some Polaroid shots and listen to instruction from the coaching staff. By that point, the Giants defense was on its feet.

Anderson added a seven-yard run and Carthon gained another three for a first down. Stopping three running backs with varying styles is a challenge for any defense, but it was especially difficult for one that had been on the field for more than 30 minutes. Early in the first quarter, Hostetler overthrew Bavaro on a wide-open seam route that should have been a touchdown. The Giants knew that Bavaro could outrun the Bills linebackers, who struggled in coverage, and called the same play from the first quarter. On the next play Bavaro caught a 19-yard pass at the Bills 27. The Giants exposed Bills safety Leonard Smith again when Ingram caught a 13-yard pass to the outside at the Bills 14.

"I thought to myself I had to keep running and just take the punishment from Smith," Bavaro said.

"All I can say is we had some blown coverages," Polian said. "And it was one of the things that frustrated Marv and [me] the most."

The Giants earned another first down from a six-yard run by Meggett. First-and-goal at the 3. The score was 19–17 Buffalo, and a Giants touchdown would force the Bills to score a touchdown to win. Bennett wasn't having it. He tackled Anderson for a four-yard loss.

Said Talley, "We were almost saying our defense wasn't dead yet. We were determined to make one last stand."

Anderson gained the four yards back on the next play, but Hostetler's pass to him fell incomplete on third down. The Giants had to settle for a chip-shot field goal, but the lead was theirs, 20–19, with only seven minutes to go.

On the Bills' next possession, they faced third-and-8 when Kelly hit Al Edwards for what appeared to be first-down yardage. But just as the ball hit Edwards' chest, Perry Williams leveled him, forcing him to drop the ball.

"Oh my God, that hit he made on Edwards. That hit he made," said Walls, holding up his hands as if only some higher power could have made the play. "Unquestionably one of the biggest plays of the game, if not the biggest. As upset as I was with Perry in the first quarter for tipping the ball and allowing Lofton to catch the pass, I couldn't have been more ecstatic when he made that play."

Perhaps Walls wanted to use his favorite expression ("C'mon, why you playing with me like that?") to ask if what he just witnessed was real. Neither Walls nor the rest of his teammates expected Williams to make that kind of a punishing play. After all, he was only 200 pounds.

Marshall, who was friends with Williams, thought maybe he could have. "That's my boy," Marshall said, trying not to laugh as he watched the hit.

Not only did the Giants out-strategize the Bills, but they were also superior in the little things. For instance, they almost never ran a play before the 35-second play clock had reached two seconds—just to be sure they consumed as much time as possible. To borrow a phrase from ESPN Classic's Brian Kenny, "mental paralysis" set in after Buffalo stopped the Giants at midfield with two minutes remaining. Hostetler only gained a yard, needing three, on a third-down bootleg. Buffalo needed to call a timeout, but they didn't do it until 13 seconds after the play was over.

"I think there was some indecision because they weren't in these situations a lot," Baxter said.

Perhaps if the Bills had those 13 extra seconds, Thomas could have gained another 10 yards on the Bills' last drive. It might have been enough to give Norwood a field-goal attempt from 40 yards or less. From 40 yards or less, Norwood was nearly automatic. He had hit 87 percent of his kicks from inside 40 yards on the season.

After the game, Parcells told several writers that he thought his punter Sean Landeta was a critical factor in the game. Of Landeta's four punts, one was a touchback and three led to fair catches—meaning Edwards, the Bills' devastating punt returner, never had the opportunity to return a kick. Landeta didn't always punt the ball the farthest, but the height of his kicks allowed the Giants special teams players plenty of time to get downfield to make the tackle. And with 2:16 left on the clock, Landeta nailed another high-spiraling kick that Edwards fair caught at the 10.

Perhaps it was Harry Kalas of NFL Films who best described Buffalo's situation as they entered their final drive. NFL Films not only provides exciting

Super Bowl narratives, but it also mythologizes them. And indeed, if there was an NFL drive that deserved some mythology, this one was it. (Tim Russert, the moderator of *Meet the Press* and avid Buffalo Bills fan, years later admitted to thinking about this drive almost every night before he went to bed.)

"Throughout the season, Buffalo had elevated the two minute drill into a complete offensive strategy. And they tried to make it work one final time, but with their passing game nonexistent, they were reduced to nothing but pure guts and will," Kalas said.

The Giants' game plan called for a mixture of five- and six-defensive back formations in two-minute situations. Belichick thought that if they could prevent the Bills from throwing, there simply wouldn't be enough time to get in scoring position—no matter how well Thomas ran. The savvy defensive coordinator, though, appeared to have underestimated the grittiness of Jim Kelly. On first down, Kelly took advantage of the linebackers' deep coverage, running for eight yards himself.

"How the hell did he escape?" Leonard asks himself when he watches the tape. "We had him contained. He found the narrowest of holes to run."

Kelly ran on second down too, but gained only a yard. Earlier, the Giants lined up in the same formation on third-and-1 and Kelly threw a crossing route to Reed. The Giants expected the same play. Unfortunately, Kelly handed off to Thomas instead, and the runner reversed left. The Giants defensive line failed to seal the left edge, leaving Thomas ample running room. He ran as fast as he could with what little stamina he had left.

"We thought he might run for a touchdown," Parcells said.

Walls sprinted from the middle of the field to the left side to make an open-field tackle at the Bills 41. It was a 22-yard gain, but it easily could have been 40.

"Without question, it might have been the biggest play of the game," Parcells said.

Added Walls, "Just another play that gave me bragging rights on a lot of the young guys."

The next play demonstrated the paradox of the Giants defense. Kelly had roughly five seconds in the pocket to survey the field.

"That's unbelievable," screamed Dierdorf from the broadcast booth.

Kelly's receivers, though, were well covered. He could only throw a four-yard pass to Reed, whom Reasons tackled immediately. It was Reed's only catch of the second half. Kelly soon learned that he was his own best friend on this series, scrambling another nine yards on the Bills' next play to the Giants 46.

"He was a great athlete running on a really tired defense. He just knew where the openings were," Marshall said.

After the run, Kelly called the Bills' final timeout. It was a beneficial timeout for the Giants, who desperately needed a defensive substitution. Nose tackle Erik Howard was huffing and puffing as he came off the field. Playing nose with only two defensive linemen was especially grueling, as two or three offensive linemen often blocked him.

"The whole night Erik and I were the only down linemen taking on such a big Buffalo offensive line. I was as tired as him. I knew how he felt. I thought about coming out, but I had told myself I wouldn't do it. Erik was a quiet player who worked his tail off. I really respected him," said Marshall.

Added Howard, "A lot of people didn't realize that I was having a full-blown asthma attack. I couldn't breathe. I had the type of asthma that was made worse by exercising and running. Thank God they called that timeout. I started seeing spots and felt very claustrophobic, like I was squished in the middle seat of a long car ride.

"It made me want to rip my uniform off. In that situation, your mind can go crazy on you, and that is what you are trying to prevent. If there was any way I could have stayed on the field, I would have.

"I remember when I was in college, feeling that I had to work twice as hard as other players. I saw an asthma brochure after practice and said to myself, *Damn, I have all the symptoms.* I went to the doctor and he diagnosed me. A few weeks after the Super Bowl, a doctor in California called me and said he wished he could have been in contact with the Giants training staff because he was watching the game and instantly recognized that I had a full-blown asthma attack."

All night, the Giants had shut down the Bills' talented tight end Keith McKeller, limiting him to just one catch.

"Carl really did a terrific job on him. He could play over the tight end as well as any linebacker I have ever seen," Marshall said.

Then McKeller caught a pass that bounced off his shoe tops and into his hands for a six-yard gain to the Giants 40. The Giants thought the pass was incomplete, thinking it bounced off the ground, but the replay clearly showed it went off McKeller's shoe top.

"Incredible concentration," Dierdorf bellowed. "Great athleticism."

The play was reviewed and upheld. It was a completion. The clock continued to tick down, and the Bills snapped the ball with 26 seconds left. Thomas ran 11 yards to the right and Mark Collins tackled him at the 29. Nineteen seconds remained.

"We told him to get down before the play started," said Polian, who was standing on the field at this point. "Because he didn't have any timeouts left, we knew that if Thurman cuts back towards the middle of the field, the game is over and we don't even get to attempt a field goal."

If Collins hadn't tackled him, Thomas probably would have escaped out of bounds or gained another couple of yards before falling to the ground.

The Bills, scrambling to stop the clock, finally spiked the ball with eight seconds left.

Polian insists the Bills couldn't have run another play. "Too risky," he said.

Kelly, though, *could* have thrown a quick out pass to the sidelines. Or, if nothing was open, he could have thrown the ball away. This sequence probably would have taken less than five seconds.

"We had this stuff figured out in advance," Levy said. "Under 10 seconds, with no timeouts left, we were going to kick the field goal."

Earlier in the week, Scott Norwood had told *Buffalo News* writer Vic Carucci that he wanted the opportunity to make a game-winning kick. Perhaps the statement was fitting, considering Buffalo's brazen overconfidence in the week leading up to the game. On Media Day, Bruce Smith said that this game would be the start of a Buffalo dynasty. If it was, they had to make this kick. Norwood told Kelly that if the Bills offense made it to the Giants 30, he could hit it.

"This whole thing about confidence is a bunch of BS," Bennett said. "Our confidence was what helped make us really good. I think what united the Giants and us is that we needed to win. We couldn't accept just losing a close game. The Giants were just as confident as we were, and they talked a lot of trash. I still see LT on the golf course today and he still gives me shit about that game and my career. I always appreciate what LT did, because he is what made football popular in the 1980s and allowed linebackers to earn a lot more money. He helped make me millions of dollars.

"I also liked the fact that we were confident because it allowed us to have fun with the opposing fans. When we went into Giants Stadium, they didn't like us very much because we weren't a blue-collar team. We were used to talking trash with the same fans at different stadiums. We almost looked forward to seeing them. Sometimes it was more fun to play on the road than at home."

"What you realized when Norwood lined up for the kick is how even [the] teams [were]. There was not a great disparity between them," said Bennett. "I always would joke that a lot of our players were similar to a lot of their players, like Carl Banks and Darryl Talley."

Norwood was only 1-for-5 on grass in his career on kicks from more than 40 yards. Grass is generally considered tougher to kick on than Astroturf, the turf on Buffalo's home field, where Norwood was used to kicking. *Sports Illustrated's* Peter King astutely notes that Norwood averaged the shortest distance on made field goals of any kicker in the AFC in 1990. Simply put, he had one of the weaker legs in the NFL. He had attempted only one kick of more than 40 yards on grass that season (against the Cleveland Browns) and missed far to the right. Before that kick, Norwood's last attempt on grass was in Chicago in 1988, where he missed wide right again.

Collins fittingly remembered earlier in the week, thinking that if the Giants held the Bills to under 20 points they would win; otherwise, they would lose.

"I am on the sidelines thinking, *Well, I made the right prediction,*" Collins said. *"Now let's just hope we fall on the right side."*

The Giants players engaged in the same ritual as they had in San Francisco a week earlier when Bahr attempted his kick. They knelt in circles and prayed. On the other sideline, the Bills players all held hands—except for Thomas and Bennett, who sat on the bench because of their exhaustion. Parcells called a timeout to ice the kicker, screaming at LT to come to the sidelines. Parcells instructed Taylor on how to block the kick.

And then the only thing left to do was watch. On the sideline, Giants special teams coach Mike Sweatman told Carthon and Johnnie Cooks that he was confident because of Norwood's low success rate on grass kicks of more than 40 yards.

Marshall still almost has tears in his eyes watching it 20 years later. He views the replay, his hands covering his face. He still looks almost bewildered—thinking it really happened in a season where the Giants seemed like an afterthought. In 1986 the Giants blew teams out. This season, however, almost every game was close. On the Giants sideline, a Disney representative told Anderson that if Norwood missed the kick he was the MVP; meanwhile, on the other sideline, Thomas was told if Norwood makes the kick, *he* was the MVP.

"That kick really epitomized the season in one play," Marshall said. "We would just find ways to win."

And when the kick landed right of the goal post, there were still four seconds left. Steve DeOssie, though, was on the field with a video camera, recording the celebration. It was the only amateur footage shot in Tampa Stadium that day, as video cameras were forbidden. DeOssie had snuck the camera into the Giants locker room several days before the game. He put a towel over it at halftime and placed it under the Giants bench just before the start of the third quarter. No one thought anything about the illegal action. Al Michaels just screamed, "Look at DeOssie!"

Parcells turned to Johnson and Banks and said, "Give me a ride," after Norwood's kick sailed wide right. Johnson was the first Giants player to hug Parcells after Norwood's miss. With the help of Marshall, Parcells was on the shoulders of his top defensive players. The coach, who finished his first season with the Giants at 3–12–1 and was only retained on a fluke, had given New York two Super Bowl victories in five years. All he could do was give thanks to the heavens above.

"You realize God plays a part in these games," Parcells told Brent Musburger afterward.

Added Howard Cross, "Maybe Parcells could have come back the next year, but he probably felt that he accomplished all that he needed to accomplish."

As he smiled and held his hands in the air, it was hard to argue.

Afterword

IT WASN'T SUPPOSED TO END THE WAY IT DID.

"We kind of had this feeling that if Bill Parcells stayed, we would win forever," said Bavaro. "We had a really young team, a young offensive line, good running backs, and two really good quarterbacks. When Parcells retired, it came as a shock to so many."

Added LT, "I always thought if Bill had stayed we could have won one more Super Bowl. He probably knew that he was leaving, but I don't think anybody on the team did. You just got the feeling we could have done more."

The Giants hired assistant offensive coordinator Ray Handley to coach the team, a man Parcells referred to as one of the brightest offensive minds he had ever seen. Parcells didn't announce his retirement until May. Several doctors' visits had revealed the existence of a heart arrhythmia.

"It was tough to admit that I really couldn't coach, and the doctors told me that. I wanted to coach, but I had a host of physical problems with my heart and everything. It was a sad day for me because of how good the Maras were to me and how much I enjoyed the experience," Parcells said.

Bavaro said, "I hate to say it, but in order to succeed in this league, you really need to be a taskmaster. You can't have the inmates running the asylum, and that is what happened with Handley. When I was in Cleveland, we came to work out with the Giants in New Jersey and it was a completely different team. I almost didn't recognize it. We used to run after practice, but not this group. They just kind of did whatever they felt like."

In 1991, the Giants finished 8–8. And after finishing a disappointing 6–10 in 1992, Handley was fired as a result. With the start of free agency in 1993, the Giants lost a lot of players, including Leonard Marshall, Carl Banks, and Pepper Johnson. Phil Simms and LT did lead the Giants to the playoffs in 1993 under Dan Reeves, but the 49ers decimated them in the divisional round of the playoffs, 44–3.

It was the end of an era. An end that had come far sooner than anyone expected.

"What made the season so special was all the doubters gave us ammunition," Parcells said. "When no one believes you could do it, it makes victory that much sweeter and that was the 1990 season."

Acknowledgments

TO STATE THE OBVIOUS, writing a book is not an easy process, but it might be more difficult on one's friends and family than the author himself. I would first like to thank Leonard Marshall for his unwavering support throughout the entire process. He has become more than a co-author, but a good friend for life.

I would like thank my agent, Ian Kleinert, who brought this project to life. I also owe a big thanks to the editor-in-chief of ESPN Books, Steve Wulf, who nurtured the project and gave me tremendous advice about not only the topic on which I was writing, but also how to write the book. A first book is difficult for any author and Steve helped make it easier. Steve was kind of enough to put me in touch with Ian.

The folks at Triumph—particularly Adam Motin and Katy Sprinkel—have been a great help. Their editing skills made this book better.

There are others who gave their time when they were incredibly busy, and I am forever thankful. Craig Mortali, a producer for ESPN, took the time to meet with me in Connecticut and share his memories from the game. He also found old artifacts in his home. Thanks to the staff at the Pro Football Hall of Fame, particularly Jason Aikens and Pete Fierle, for their help when I visited Canton, Ohio, to view Bill Belichick's game plan.

To the director of NFL public relations, Greg Aiello, for always being there when approval was needed on various requests—and also to Joe Browne for always making me feel welcome. Thanks to Steve Sabol of NFL Films who shared his insights about the 1990 season and Super Bowl XXV.

To Bill Parcells for writing the forward and giving me two long exclusive interviews and to all the players interviewed for this project. Special thanks to Everson Walls, who allowed me to spend a full day with him in Tampa, Florida, prior to Super Bowl XXLIII.

I have some incredible friends who helped me believe this project could become a reality. Without them, I am not sure this would have happened. To *Boston Herald* columnist Ron Borges, who always answered my calls and told me to stay disciplined by only writing a certain amount each day. This approach allowed me to feel like I was accomplishing something amid all the chaos.

To my mentors from ESPN, John Clayton and Len Pasquarelli, and to Peter King of *Sports Illustrated*. Each of them has never hesitated to answer a question of mine or provide helpful feedback on an article I had written. Special thanks to good friend Aris Bidianos for letting me stay with him when I had to do research in New York.

I was fortunate to find such a helpful staff at the New York Public Library, where I spent over 100 hours on three separate trips doing research for this project. The hundreds of rolls of microfilm were instrumental in providing a narrative for this project. Joey Stein provided additional research help.

I owe a deep debt of gratitude to Barry Meisel and Gary Myers, who covered the 1990 Giants for the *Daily News*. Myers, to this day, remains one of the best NFL writers in the business. Thanks also to Steve Serby, Hank Gola, and Jerry Izenberg, whose articles appeared in the *New York Post*, for their terrific coverage of the Giants in a locker room that was often difficult for the media to navigate.

Thank you to the staff at the Pro Football Hall of Fame for providing me with numerous articles from across the country about Super Bowl XXV in addition to their assistance with Bill Belichick's game plan. Their collection was terrific. The remainder of my research relied on interviews with more than 50 folks related to the game—players, coaches, reporters, and executives. I owe them all a deep debt of gratitude.

I have a tremendous family. Thanks to my little brother, Daniel, for always keeping me humble by never failing to remind me, "everyone writes a book." To my other brother, Michael, for his support. And I am forever indebted to my parents, who listened to my complaints on the project's most difficult days.

My father's fascination with Super Bowl XXV eventually rubbed off on me. When it was originally aired, I was five and uninterested in football. My father told my mother he didn't think I would ever be a football fan.

Well, I guess some predictions are meant to be proven wrong.

One prediction, though, that I think will hold true into the future is I will continue to have great friends and family.

—W.B.

To my kids, Erika Christina and Arianna Nicole.

To my parents and family for putting up with me since my departure from the NFL.

To my teammates Lawrence Taylor, Phil Simms, Harry Carson, Pepper Johnson, Jimmy Burt, Carl Banks. and Perry Williams.

To others who embraced No. 70 and shared such special moments in Giants history.

And finally, to the woman who makes me go, my soul mate. You've been there for me in more ways than one, and for this I will always love you.

God Bless!

—L.M.

Appendix 1: The Season

Week 1: Philadelphia Eagles (0–0) at New York Giants (0–0)
September 9, 1990
Giants Stadium (Attendance: 76,202)

Philadelphia	3	7	0	10	20
New York	6	0	14	7	27

Scoring Plays:
NYG—Allegre 38-yard FG
NYG—Allegre 46-yard FG
PHI—Ruzek 37-yard FG
PHI—Toney 18-yard pass from Byars (Ruzek PAT)
NYG—Hampton 12-yard pass from Simms (Allegre PAT)
NYG—Meggett 68-yard punt return (Allegre PAT)
PHI—Cunningham 1-yard rush (Ruzek PAT)
PHI—Ruzek 29-yard FG

Leading Rushers: NYG—Tillman, 15-39. PHI—Toney 13-50
Leading Receivers: NYG—Carthon, 4-33. PHI—Byars 7-60

Giants quarterback Phil Simms threw two touchdown passes as the Giants ended their four-game losing streak to their division rival, the Philadelphia Eagles. Cornerback Everson Walls made a grand entrance in his first game as a Giant, picking off a Randall Cunningham pass on the Giants' first possession. New York pulled away in the second half when quarterback Phil Simms threw a 12-yard touchdown pass to Rodney Hampton and Dave Meggett returned a punt for a touchdown. Simms added a 41-yard touchdown pass to Mark Ingram in the fourth quarter to give the Giants a 27–10 lead. The Eagles scored 10 fourth-quarter points, but a Randall Cunningham Hail Mary fell just short to end the game.

Week 2: New York Giants (1–0) at Dallas Cowboys (1–0)

September 16, 1990

Texas Stadium (Attendance: 61,090)

New York	0	14	7	7	28
Dallas	0	7	0	0	7

Scoring Plays:

NYG—Simms 4-yard run (Allegre PAT)

NYG—Anderson 1-yard run (Allegre PAT)

DAL—Wright 90-yard kickoff return (Willis PAT)

NYG—Bavaro 4-yard pass from Simms (Allegre PAT)

NYG—Taylor 11-yard interception return (Allegre PAT)

Leading Rushers: NYG—Tillman, 22-71. DAL—E. Smith, 6-11

Leading Receivers: NYG—Bavaro, 5-72. DAL—Awalt, 3-35

The game conditions were sweltering, as temperatures topped out at 96 degrees in Dallas. Despite fumbling at the Cowboys 1 on their opening possession, Phil Simms still led the Giants on two long touchdown drives in the second quarter. LT's interception return in the fourth quarter was the nail in the coffin. The Cowboys offense failed to score at all, the team's sole points coming on special teams.

Week 3: Miami Dolphins (2–0) at New York Giants (2–0)

September 23, 1990

Giants Stadium (Attendance: 76,483)

Miami	0	0	3	0	3
New York	3	7	0	10	20

Scoring Plays:

NYG—Allegre 22-yard FG

NYG—Anderson 1-yard run (Allegre PAT)

MIA—Stoyanovich 51-yard FG

NYG—Anderson 2-yard run (Allegre PAT)

NYG—Allegre 45-yard FG

Leading Rushers: NYG—Anderson, 25-72. MIA—Secules, 1-16

Leading Receivers: NYG—Meggett, 4-93. Clayton, 5-41

The two clubs met for the first time in the regular season since 1972 and it wasn't much of a competition when they did. Miami quarterback Dan Marino threw for only 115 yards and tossed up two interceptions. The Giants defense punished the Miami receivers all day. The Giants scored their second touchdown when Perry Williams leveled Dolphins WR Mark Clayton on a completed pass and LT picked up the ball and returned it to the 11. Four plays later, Ottis Anderson found the end zone.

Week 4: Dallas Cowboys (1–2) at New York Giants (3–0)

September 30, 1990

Giants Stadium (Attendance: 75,923)

Dallas	0	3	7	7	17
New York	7	10	0	14	31

Scoring Plays:

NYG—Ingram 12-yard pass from Simms (Bahr PAT)

DAL—Willis 22-yard FG

NYG—Bahr 34-yard FG

NYG—Mrosko 7-yard pass from Simms (Bahr PAT)

DAL—Smith 5-yard run (Willis PAT)

NYG—Hampton 24-yard pass from Simms (Bahr PAT)

NYG—Hostetler 12-yard run (Bahr PAT)

DAL—Novacek 7-yard pass from Aikman (Willis PAT)

Leading Rushers: NYG—Anderson, 17-79. DAL—E. Smith, 12- 28

Leading Receivers: NYG—Hampton, 4-65. DAL—Novacek, 9-85

The Giants improved their record to 4–0 with their second win over the Cowboys in just three weeks. After Steve DeOssie recovered a fumble in the first quarter, Phil Simms hit Mark Ingram for a 12-yard touchdown pass to give the Giants a 7–0 lead. The Giants took a 17–3 halftime lead when Simms hit reserve tight end Bob Mrosko for a seven-yard touchdown pass. Simms added a 29-yard touchdown pass to rookie running back Rodney Hampton in the second half. In reserve duty, backup quarterback Jeff Hostetler added six points on a 12-yard run.

Week 6: New York Giants (4–0) at Washington Redskins (3–1)
October 14, 1990
RFK Stadium (Attendance: 54,737)

New York	0	7	14	3	24
Washington	3	0	10	7	20

Scoring Plays:
WAS—Lohmiller 42-yard FG
NYG—Baker 80-yard pass from Simms (Bahr PAT)
WAS—Lohmiller 35-yard FG
NYG—Anderson 5-yard run (Bahr PAT)
WAS—31-yard pass from Byner (Lohmiller PAT)
NYG—Bavaro 2-yard pass from Simms (Bahr PAT)
WAS—Riggs 1-yard run (Lohmiller PAT)
NYG—Bahr 19-yard FG

Leading Rushers: NYG—Anderson, 18-40. WAS—Riggs 18-61
Leading Receivers: NYG—Baker, 3-109. WAS—Sanders 2-48

The Giants squeaked past the Redskins in their closest victory of the season to date. It was Big Blue's fifth consecutive win over their division rivals. The Giants found their first huge play when Phil Simms hit Stephen Baker for an 80-yard touchdown on a crossing pattern. With a 7–6 lead early in the third quarter, Simms found Mark Bavaro for a 61-yard pass play. Anderson gave the Giants a 14–6 lead two plays later. Washington scored to bring them within one point, but then Simms completed a 63-yard pass play to Maurice Carthon that set up a short touchdown pass to Bavaro. With the score 24–21 and Washington driving, Greg Jackson intercepted a pass to end any hope of a Redskins comeback.

Week 7: Phoenix Cardinals (2–3) at New York Giants (5–0)

October 21, 1990

Giants Stadium (Attendance: 76,518)

Phoenix	3	7	6	3	19
New York	7	3	0	10	20

Scoring Plays:

NYG—Anderson 4-yard run (Bahr PAT)

PHO—Del Greco 39-yard FG

NYG—Bahr 34-yard FG

PHO—Sharpe 1-yard pass from Rosenbach (Del Greco PAT)

PHO—Del Greco 18-yard FG

PHO—Del Greco 34-yard FG

PHO—Del Greco 45-yard FG

NYG—Baker 38-yard pass from Hostetler (Bahr PAT)

NYG—Bahr 40-yard FG

Leading Rushers: NYG—Anderson, 11-88. PHO—Johnson, 30-108
Leading Receivers: NYG—Baker 3-65. PHO—Proehl, 2-33

The Giants barely survived against the lowly Cardinals. They snuck away with a victory thanks to a heroic comeback from backup quarterback Jeff Hostetler, who came in for an injured Phil Simms at the end of the first quarter. When Hostetler fumbled in the fourth quarter, with the Cardinals leading 19–10, it looked like the Giants' undefeated record would come to an end. Hostetler, however, led the Giants on an eight-play, 76-yard drive, capped off by 38-yard touchdown pass to Stephen Baker. After the Giants defense forced a three-and-out, Hostetler drove the Giants 50 yards and Matt Bahr hit a 40-yard field goal to give the Giants the game.

Week 8: Washington Redskins (4–2) at New York Giants (6–0)
October 28, 1990
Giants Stadium (Attendance: 75,321)

Washington	0	3	7	0	10
New York	0	14	0	7	21

Scoring Plays:
NYG—Baker 4-yard pass from Simms (Bahr PAT)
NYG—Bavaro 13-yard pass from Simms (Bahr PAT)
WAS—Lohmiller 45-yard FG
WAS—Humphries 5-yard run (Lohmiller PAT)
NYG—Walls 28-yard interception return (Bahr PAT)

Leading Rushers: NYG—Anderson, 24-92. WAS—Byner, 9-22
Leading Receivers: NYG—Bavaro, 3-32. WAS—Warren 10-66

The Giants handled the Redskins for the second time in three weeks. Phil Simms threw two touchdowns in the second quarter—one to Stephen Baker and the other to Mark Bavaro—to own a 14–3 at the half. After a Redskins touchdown in the third quarter that brought Washington within a score, cornerback Everson Walls closed the door. Walls ended any hope of a Redskins comeback when he completed his career-first interception for a touchdown. The Giants stretched their lead to 21–10 and never looked back. New York was now 7–0.

Week 9: New York Giants (7–0) at Indianapolis Colts (2–5)

November 5, 1990

Hoosier Dome (Attendance: 58,688)

New York	3	14	0	7	24
Indianapolis	0	0	7	0	7

Scoring Plays:

NYG—Bahr 23-yard FG

NYG—Anderson 2-yard run (Bahr PAT)

NYG—Anderson 3-yard run (Bahr PAT)

IND—Bentley 1-yard run (Biasucci PAT)

NYG—Duerson 31-yard fumble return (Bahr PAT)

Leading Rushers: NYG—Anderson, 14-55. IND—Bentley, 8-29

Leading Receivers: NYG—Meggett, 6-47. IND—Morgan, 3-53

On the Giants' first Monday night game of the year, they raced out to a 17–0 halftime lead. The Giants put together consecutive touchdown drives in the second quarter behind the running of Ottis Anderson and Lewis Tillman. The Giants played conservatively in the second half, adding only 7 points when Pepper Johnson stripped Colts quarterback Jeff George of the ball and Dave Duerson returned the fumble 31 yards for a touchdown (and subsequent extra point by Bahr).

Week 10: New York Giants (8–0) at Los Angeles Rams (3–5)
November 11, 1990
Anaheim Stadium (Attendance: 64,632)

New York	3	7	7	14	31
Los Angeles	0	0	7	0	7

Scoring Plays:
NYG—Bahr 44-yard FG
NYG—Bavaro 9-yard pass from Simms (Bahr PAT)
LA—Gary 3-yard run (Lansford PAT)
NYG—Hampton 19-yard run (Bahr PAT)
NYG—Anderson 3-yard run (Bahr PAT)
NYG—Tillman 1-yard run (Bahr PAT)

Leading Rushers: NYG—Anderson, 18-60. LA—Gary, 13-44
Leading Receivers: Ingram, 3-60. LA—Holohan, 4-40

The Giants arrived in Anaheim smelling blood, eager to avenge their overtime divisional playoff loss to the Rams in the previous postseason. The Giants shut out Los Angeles in the first half while building a 10–0 lead. The Rams cut the lead to three after Rams linebacker Kevin Greene stripped Phil Simms. The turnover ultimately led to a Cleveland Gray touchdown run. The Giants answered back with a Rodney Hampton rushing touchdown. New York scored 14 points in the fourth quarter, including a touchdown off a Gary Reasons interception of Rams quarterback Jim Everett deep in Rams territory. New York improved to 9–0, despite a short week of preparation and a cross-country flight.

Week 11: Detroit Lions (3–6) at New York Giants (9–0)

November 18, 1990

Giants Stadium (Attendance: 76,109)

Detroit	0	0	0	0	0
New York	7	13	0	0	20

Scoring Plays:

NYG—Baker 33-yard pass from Simms (Bahr PAT)

NYG—Bahr 24-yard FG

NYG—Ingram 57-yard pass from Simms (Bahr PAT)

NYG—Bahr 49-yard FG

Leading Rushers: NYG—Anderson 23-91. DET—Sanders, 11-69

Leading Receivers: NYG—Manuel, 2-25. DET—Johnson, 7-61

The Giants defense shut down the Lions run-and-shoot offense to earn their first shutout of the season. Defensive coordinator Bill Belichick used a nickel defense to get more speed on the field. The Giants held Pro Bowl Lions running back Barry Sanders to just 69 yards on 11 carries. New York demonstrated a balanced offense as the defense held their ground. All was quiet in the second half, as both teams were held scoreless.

Week 12: New York Giants (10–0) at Philadelphia Eagles (6–4)

November 25, 1990

Veterans Stadium (Attendance: 66,706)

New York	7	6	0	0	13
Philadelphia	7	7	3	14	31

Scoring Plays:

NYG—Ingram 15-yard pass from Simms (Bahr PAT)

PHI—Barnett 49-yard pass from Cunningham (Ruzek PAT)

PHI—Cunningham 1-yard run (Ruzek PAT)

NYG—Bavaro 4-yard pass from Simms (PAT failed)

PHI—Ruzek 39-yard FG

PHI—Williams 6-yard pass from Cunningham (Ruzek PAT)

PHI—Evans 23-yard interception return (Ruzek PAT)

Leading Rushers: NYG—Meggett, 2-61. PHI—Sherman, 21-71

Leading Recivers: NYG—Baker, 3-65. PHI—Byars, 8-128

Phil Simms threw a 15-yard touchdown pass to Mark Ingram in the first quarter to give the Giants a 7-0 lead. Then Randall Cunningham responded with a 49-yard touchdown pass to Fred Barnett to knot the score at seven. Philadelphia went 80 yards on 16 plays in the second quarter to take a 14–7 lead. The Giants responded with a touchdown of their own, but Matt Bahr missed the extra point. Philadelphia took the one-point lead into halftime. In the second half, the Eagles defense was punishing, holding the Giants scoreless. Meanwhile, Cunningham led the Eagles on another long touchdown drive and the defense then sealed the victory when Clyde Simmons deflected a Phil Simms pass and Byron Evans returned it 22 yards for a touchdown.

Week 13: New York Giants (10–1) at San Francisco (10–1)

December 3, 1990

Candlestick Park (Attendance: 66,092)

New York	0	3	0	0	0
San Francisco	0	7	0	0	7

Scoring Plays:

NYG—Bahr 20-yard FG

SF—Taylor 23-yard pass from Montana (Cofer PAT)

Leading Rushers: NYG—Anderson, 19-39. SF—Carter, 12-19

Leading Receivers: NYG—Bavaro, 3-43. SF—Taylor, 3-38

Both teams came into the game at 10-1 and the winner would likely receive home-field advantage in the playoffs. The highly anticipated affair was expected to be a shootout, but the game turned out to be a defensive struggle. The Giants took a 3–0 lead early in the second quarter, and the 49ers quickly responded on the ensuing series as Roger Craig ran 31 yards to the Giants 28 to set up a 23-yard touchdown pass to John Taylor. The Giants drove inside the 49ers 10 in the fourth quarter, but the 49ers defense made the goal-line stand, holding New York on four consecutive downs.

Week 14: Minnesota Vikings (6–6) at New York (10–2)

December 9, 1990

Giants Stadium (Attendance: 76,121)

Minnesota	5	7	3	0	15
New York	3	7	0	13	23

Scoring Plays:

MIN—Doleman sack of Simms for safety

MIN—Reveiz 22-yard FG

NYG—Bahr 36-yard FG

MIN—Anderson 1-yard run (Reveiz PAT)

NYG—Anderson 1-yard run (Bahr PAT)

MIN—Reveiz 37-yard FG

NYG—Bahr 49-yard FG

NYG—Anderson 2-yard run (Bahr PAT)

NYG—Bahr 18-yard FG

Leading Rushers: NYG—Hampton, 19-78. MIN—Walker, 15-78

Leading Receivers: NYG—Baker, 3-57. MIN—Jordan, 5-70

After an anemic first half in which the Giants trailed 12–10 at halftime, New York played a nearly flawless second half, giving up only a field goal. They trailed 15-10 heading into the fourth quarter when Greg Jackson intercepted Rich Gannon. The turnover led to a Giants field goal. Ottis Anderson added six more, and the Giants overtook the lead. They sealed the victory when Gary Reasons intercepted a Gannon pass at the Vikings 17. Matt Bahr's field goal made it 23–15, the final score. The Giants snapped their two-game losing streak and clinched their second-straight NFC East title.

Week 15: Buffalo Bills (11–2) at New York Giants (11–2)

December 15, 1990

Giants Stadium (Attendance: 66,893)

Buffalo	7	7	0	3	17
New York	7	3	3	0	13

Scoring Plays:

NYG—Anderson 1-yard run (Bahr PAT)

BUF—Reed 6-yard pass from Kelly (Norwood PAT)

BUF—Thomas 2-yard run (Norwood PAT)

NYG—Bahr 23-yard FG

NYG—Bahr 22-yard FG

BUF—Norwood 29-yard FG

Leading Rushers: NYG—Hampton, 21-105. BUF—Thomas 21-105

Leading Receivers: NYG—Baker, 4-56. BUF—Thomas, 4-65

The rainy weather provided a fitting backdrop for the mood of both teams as each lost their quarterback to injury in NBC's Saturday Game of the Week. Rodney Hampton's 41-yard run on the Giants opening drive helped them take an early lead. The Bills, though, answered quickly with a six-play, 74-yard drive capped by a six-yard touchdown pass to Andre Reed. The Bills took a 14-7 lead when Thurman Thomas ran for a two-yard touchdown. An exchange of field goals made the score 17–13 in the fourth quarter when backup quarterback Jeff Hostetler led the Giants to the Bills 26—but New York failed to make a first down in four tries and fell short.

Week 16: New York Giants (11–3) at Phoenix Cardinals (5–10)
December 23, 1990
Sun Devil Stadium (Attendance: 41,212)

New York	3	7	7	7	24
Phoenix	0	7	7	7	21

Scoring Plays:
NYG—Bahr 27-yard FG
NYG—Hampton 2-yard run (Bahr PAT)
PHO—Flagler 11-yard pass from Rosenbach (Del Greco PAT)
NYG—Ingram 44-yard pass from Hostetler (Bahr PAT)
PHO—Jones 68-yard pass from Rosenbach (Del Greco PAT)
NYG—Hostetler 4-yard run (Bahr PAT)
PHO—Proehl 3-yard pass from Rosenbach (Del Greco PAT)

Leading Rushers: NYG—Carthon, 12-67. PHO—Johnson, 15-50
Leading Receivers: Ingram, 4-98. PHO—Green, 8-147

In his first start of the season, backup quarterback Jeff Hostetler turned out to be the least of the Giants' worries. The Giants jumped out to a 10–0 lead thanks to a Rodney Hampton touchdown. The Cardinals closed the gap to three just before halftime. In the second half, Hostetler hit Mark Ingram for a long touchdown pass to stretch the lead, but Arizona responded with a big play of its own when quarterback Timm Rosenbach found Ernie Jones on a crossing pattern for a 68-yard touchdown. The teams exchanged touchdowns in the fourth quarter and Arizona recovered an onside kick with less than two minutes remaining. An LT sack leveled the Cardinals' hopes for a comeback. And with that, the Giants had clinched a first-round bye in the playoffs.

Week 17: New York Giants (12–3) at New England Patriots (1–14)

December 30, 1990

Foxboro Stadium (Attendance: 60,410)

New York	10	3	0	0	13
New England	0	10	0	0	10

Scoring Plays:

NYG—Meggett 17-yard pass from Hostetler (Bahr PAT)

NYG—Bahr 44-yard FG

NE—Fryar 40-yard pass from Hodson (Staurovsky PAT)

NE—Staurovsky 19-yard FG

NYG—Bahr 27-yard FG

Leading Rushers: NYG—Hostetler, 10-82. NE—Stephens, 19-81

Leading Receivers: NYG—Ingram, 3-42. NE—Fryar, 3-54

In a contest that seemed more like a home game than a road contest, with numerous Giants fans making the three-and-a-half hour trip up I-95, Hostetler completed a 17-yard touchdown pass to Dave Meggett on the Giants' opening possession, and a Matt Bahr field goal made the score 10-0. The Patriots responded as quarterback Tommy Hodson hit Irving Fryar for a 40-yard touchdown pass to edge within three. Later in the second quarter, New England tied the score at 10. After the Giants recovered a fumbled snap just before the half deep inside Patriots territory, Matt Bahr added on three points. The second half was little more than an exchange of punts. The Patriots looked to tie late in the fourth quarter, but Staurovsky missed the kick and the Giants took over on downs and ran out the clock.

NFC Divisional Playoff: Chicago Bears at New York Giants

January 13, 1991

Giants Stadium (Attendance: 77,025)

Chicago	0	3	0	0	3
New York	10	7	7	7	31

Scoring Plays:

NYG—Bahr 46-yard FG

NYG—Baker 21-yard pass from Hostetler (Bahr PAT)

CHI—Butler 33-yard FG

NYG—Cross 5-yard pass from Hostetler (Bahr PAT)

NYG—Hostetler 3-yard run (Bahr PAT)

NYG—Carthon 1-yard run (Bahr PAT)

Leading Rushers: NYG—Anderson, 21-80. CHI—Anderson, 12-19

Leading Receivers: NYG—Baker, 3-58. CHI—Anderson, 4-23

The Giants won their first postseason game since they won Super Bowl XXI four years earlier—and they did it in convincing fashion. Leading 3-0 in the first quarter, Jeff Hostetler completed two long passes to Stephen Baker including a 21-yard TD pass on the scoring drive. The Giants defense made their biggest play of the day in the second quarter, stuffing the Bears on fourth-and-goal from the 1-yard line. Later in the quarter, Hostetler led the Giants on another long touchdown drive. The Giants led by 14 at the half, and scored two more unanswered touchdowns in the second half.

NFC Championship Game: New York Giants at San Francisco 49ers

January 20, 1991

Candlestick Park (Attendance: 65,750)

New York	3	3	3	6	15
San Francisco	3	3	7	0	13

Scoring Plays:

SF—Cofer 47-yard FG

NYG—Bahr 28-yard FG

NYG—Bahr 42-yard FG

SF—Cofer 35-yard FG

SF—Taylor 61-yard pass from Montana (Cofer PAT)

NYG—Bahr 46-yard FG

NYG—Bahr 38-yard FG

NYG—Bahr 42-yard FG

Leading Rushers: NYG—Anderson, 20-67; SF—Craig, 8-26

Leading Receivers: NYG—Ingram, 5-82; SF—Taylor, 2-75

A seesaw affair and defensive struggle in the first half, the 49ers took a 13–6 lead on a 61-yard pass from Joe Montana to John Taylor, the game's only touchdown. Trailing by four in the fourth quarter, the Giants faked a punt on fourth-and-2 and linebacker Gary Reasons ran 30 yards for a first down. A resulting Matt Bahr field goal pulled the Giants to within one point. With 2:36 left to play, the 49ers needed just one first down to run out the clock. But defensive lineman Erik Howard jarred the ball loose from Roger Craig and LT recovered, handing possession back to New York. Two big completions from Hostetler to Stephen Baker and Mark Ingram put the Giants in field goal range before Bahr hit the game-winner with no time left on the clock to send the Giants to the Super Bowl.

Super Bowl XXV: New York Giants vs. Buffalo Bills

January 27, 1991

Tampa Stadium: (73,813)

New York	3	7	7	3	20
New York	3	7	7	3	20
Buffalo	3	9	0	7	19

Scoring Plays:

NYG—Bahr 28-yard FG

BUF—Norwood 23-yard FG

BUF—Smith 1-yard run (Norwood PAT)

BUF—Safety, Smith tackles Hostetler in end zone

NYG—Baker 14-yard pass from Hostetler (Bahr PAT)

NYG—Anderson 1-yard run (Bahr PAT)

BUF—Thomas 31-yard run (Norwood PAT)

NYG—Bahr 21-yard FG

Leading Rushers: NYG—Anderson, 21-102. BUF—Thomas, 15-135

Leading Receivers: NYG—Ingram, 5-74. BUF—Reed, 8-62

The Giants game plan for controlling the clock proved successful as they held the ball for over 40 minutes in the game. The Bills took a 12–3 in the first half after a Bruce Smith safety. The Giants, though, responded with an impressive 87-yard touchdown drive, capped off by a 14-yard TD pass to Stephen Baker, before the first half elapsed. The Giants opened the third quarter with the longest touchdown drive in Super Bowl history (9:29) to take a five-point lead. The Bills overtook the lead on a Thurman Thomas touchdown rush, but the Giants marched back downfield. When Bills kicker Scott Norwood missed a 47-yard field goal with four seconds remaining, the Giants had their second Super Bowl win in franchise history.

Appendix 2:
The Team

No.	Name	Pos	G	GS	Wt, Ht
51	Bobby Abrams	LB	16	0	6'3", 240
2	Raul Allegre	K	3	0	5'9", 165
24	Ottis Anderson*	RB	16	11	6'2", 220
9	Matt Bahr*	K	13	0	5'10", 175
85	Stephen Baker*	WR	16	8	5'8", 160
58	Carl Banks*	LB	9	8	6'4", 235
89	Mark Bavaro*	TE	15	15	6'4", 245
46	Roger Brown	DB	5	0	6'0", 196
44	Maurice Carthon*	RB	16	13	6'1", 225
25	Mark Collins*	DB	13	12	5'10", 196
98	Johnie Cooks*	LB	14	6	6'4", 247
87	Howard Cross*	TE	16	8	6'5", 270
99	Steve DeOssie*	LB	16	13	6'2", 248
77	Eric Dorsey*	DE	16	11	6'5", 280
26	Dave Duerson	DB	16	2	6'1", 207
76	Jumbo Elliott*	T	8	8	6'7", 308
93	Mike Fox	DE-DT-NT	16	0	6'8", 285
29	Myron Guyton*	DB	16	16	6'1", 205
27	Rodney Hampton	RB	15	2	5'11", 221
15	Jeff Hostetler	QB	16	2	6'3", 215
74	Erik Howard*	NT-DT-DE	16	16	6'4", 275
82	Mark Ingram*	WR	16	14	5'10", 194
47	Greg Jackson*	DB	14	14	6'1", 217
52	Pepper Johnson*	LB	16	16	6'3", 250
61	Bob Kratch*	G	14	10	6'3", 288
84	Troy Kyles	WR	9	0	6'1", 185

* denotes starter

College/Univ	Age	Yrs	Drafted (tm/rnd/yr)
Michigan	23	Rookie	Undrafted
Montana; Texas	31	7	Undrafted
Miami (FL)	33	11	St. Louis Cardinals / 1st / 8th pick / 1979
Penn State	34	11	Pittsburgh Steelers / 6th / 165th pick / 1979
Fresno State	26	3	New York Giants / 3rd / 83rd pick / 1987
Michigan State	28	6	New York Giants / 1st / 3rd pick / 1984
Notre Dame	27	5	New York Giants / 4th / 100th pick / 1985
Virginia Tech	24	Rookie	Green Bay Packers / 8th / 215th pick / 1990
Arkansas State	29	5	Undrafted
Cal State-Fullerton	26	4	New York Giants / 2nd / 44th pick / 1986
Mississippi State	32	8	Baltimore Colts / 1st / 2nd pick / 1982
Alabama	23	1	New York Giants / 6th / 158th pick / 1989
Boston College	28	6	Dallas Cowboys / 4th / 110th pick / 1984
Notre Dame	26	4	New York Giants / 1st / 19th pick / 1986
Notre Dame	30	7	Chicago Bears / 3rd / 64th pick / 1983
Michigan	25	2	New York Giants / 2nd / 36th pick / 1988
West Virginia	23	Rookie	New York Giants / 2nd / 51st pick / 1990
Eastern Kentucky	23	1	New York Giants / 8th / 218th pick / 1989
Georgia	21	Rookie	New York Giants / 1st / 24th pick / 1990
Penn State; West Virginia	29	5	New York Giants / 3rd / 59th pick / 1984
Washington State	26	4	New York Giants / 2nd / 46th pick / 1986
Michigan State	25	3	New York Giants / 1st / 28th pick / 1987
LSU	24	1	New York Giants / 3rd / 78th pick / 1989
Ohio State	26	4	New York Giants / 2nd / 51st pick / 1986
Iowa	24	1	New York Giants / 3rd / 64th pick / 1989
Howard	22	Rookie	Undrafted

No.	Name	Pos	G	GS	Wt, Ht
5	Sean Landeta*	P	16	0	6'0", 215
86	Lionel Manuel	WR	14	0	5'11", 178
70	Leonard Marshall*	DE-DT	16	6	6'3", 288
57	Larry McGrew	LB	11	1	6'5", 233
30	Dave Meggett*	RB	16	1	5'7", 190
60	Eric Moore*	G-T	15	14	6'5", 293
80	Bob Mrosko	TE	16	2	6'6", 265
65	Bart Oates*	C	16	16	6'4", 275
55	Gary Reasons	LB	16	3	6'4", 235
64	Tom Rehder	T-G	8	0	6'7", 280
72	Doug Riesenberg*	T	16	16	6'5", 280
66	William Roberts*	G-T	16	16	6'5", 291
81	Stacy Robinson	WR	5	0	5'11", 186
22	Lee Rouson	RB	16	0	6'1", 220
11	Phil Simms*	QB	14	14	6'3", 216
56	Lawrence Taylor*	LB	16	16	6'3", 237
21	Reyna Thompson*	DB	16	4	6'0", 194
34	Lewis Tillman	RB	16	3	6'0", 204
83	Odessa Turner	WR	4	3	6'3", 205
28	Everson Walls*	DB	16	16	6'1", 194
73	John Washington*	DE-NT	16	13	6'4", 280
95	Kent Wells	DT	6	0	6'4", 295
43	Dave Whitmore	DB	16	0	6'0", 232
59	Brian S. Williams	C	16	1	6'5", 305
23	Perry Williams	DB	16	2	6'2", 203

* denotes starter

College/Univ	Age	Yrs	Drafted (tm/rnd/yr)
Towson State	28	5	Undrafted
Pacific	28	6	New York Giants / 7th / 171st pick / 1984
LSU	29	7	New York Giants / 2nd / 37th pick / 1983
USC	33	10	New England Patriots / 2nd / 45th pick / 1980
Morgan State; Towson State	24	1	New York Giants / 5th / 132nd pick / 1989
Indiana	25	2	New York Giants / 1st / 10th pick / 1988
Penn State	25	1	Houston Oilers / 9th / 244th pick / 1989
BYU	32	5	Undrafted
Northwest State (LA)	28	6	New York Giants / 4th / 105th pick / 1984
Notre Dame	25	2	New England Patriots / 3rd / 69th pick / 1988
California	25	3	New York Giants / 6th / 168th pick / 1987
Ohio State	28	6	New York Giants / 1st / 27th pick / 1984
North Dakota State Prairie View	28	5	New York Giants / 2nd / 46th pick / 1985
Colorado	28	5	New York Giants / 8th / 213th pick / 1985
Morehead State	36	11	New York Giants / 1st / 7th pick / 1979
North Carolina	31	9	New York Giants / 1st / 2nd pick / 1981
Baylor	27	4	Miami Dolphins / 9th / 247th pick / 1986
Jackson State	24	1	New York Giants / 4th / 93rd pick / 1989
Northwest State (LA)	26	3	New York Giants / 4th / 112th pick / 1987
Grambling State	31	9	Undrafted
Oklahoma State	27	4	New York Giants / 3rd / 73rd pick / 1986
Nebraska	23	Rookie	Washington Redskins / 6th / 160th pick / 1990
Stephen F. Austin	23	Rookie	New York Giants / 4th / 107th pick / 1990
Minnesota	24	1	New York Giants / 1st / 18th pick / 1989
North Carolina State	29	6	New York Giants / 7th / 178th pick / 1983

Photos

Index